To Ruth —

May heaven blessings be your constant abiding heritge. Agapé, prayers, and blessings. In Jesus' dear name,

R. Gary Heikkila

Matt. 11:28
Matt. 6:33

From Hollywood To Calvary

One Man's Religious Journey

RUSSELL GARY HEIKKILA

WestBow Press
A Division of Thomas Nelson

Author photo taken by Carolyn Kumuda, Kumuda Photography, Gardner, MA.

WestBow Press books may be ordered through booksellers or by contacting:
WestBow Press
A Division of Thomas Nelson
1663 Liberty Drive
Bloomington, IN 47403
www.westbowpress.com
1-(866) 928-1240

ISBN: 978-1-4497-6781-5 (sc)
ISBN: 978-1-4497-6780-8 (hc)
ISBN: 978-1-4497-6779-2 (e)

Library of Congress Control Number: 2012917554

Printed in the United States of America
WestBow Press rev. date: 9/28/2012

Contents

Dedication

In loving and cherished memory of my parents, Wallace and Agnes Carlson Heikkila, and to my sister, Janice, a unique woman who serves in a variety of church and community organizations. She continues to bless and encourage me in this pilgrim way.

This book is also dedicated with affection and gratitude to the four congregations I have served for almost four decades: Mission Street Congregational Church, Gardner, Massachusetts; Mission Evangelical Congregational Church, Maynard, Massachusetts; Main Street Meeting House, New Ipswich, New Hampshire, later to become the Vineyard Christian Fellowship in Rindge, New Hampshire. I am currently serving as Associate Pastor of the Elm Street Community Church in Fitchburg, MA. Your names are engraved on my heart and will forever bless my deepest soul.

But primarily to the glory of the triune God: "Oh, magnify the Lord with me, and let us exalt his name together" (Psalm 34:3).

A special thank you to all of you who have continued to encourage me over the years to "keep on keeping on" and who have urged me to write my story. To the great pastors and teachers whose wonderful sermons have been absorbed into my thinking as my own, and through my ministry, into countless lives.

R. G. H.

Preface

Many, many years have passed since I ventured to Hollywood. On March 19, 1957, the Associated Press announced that a young seminarian, Russell Gary Heikkila, of Chattanooga, Tennessee would go to Hollywood as a contender for the role of Christ in the 20th Century-Fox proposed epic, *The Greatest Story Ever Told.* My story has taken me all the way from Hope Street in the Celluloid City to Mission Street in the kingdom of God—and that has been a journey!

Today I received a residual check from Paramount Pictures for a film in which I appeared as a minister for Otto Preminger, *Tell Me You Love Me, Junie Moon.* I also appeared as a Roman Catholic priest in Otto Preminger's *The Cardinal.* That all happened many years ago; however, it brought back a flood of memories about my wilderness experience and the ultimate joy of finding meaning, purpose, and fulfillment in Gardner, Massachusetts's "little church around the corner" on Mission Street for thirty-five years prior to my semi-retirement.

Major newspapers heralded the news: "Minister Leaves Tennessee Temple to Go to Hollywood." It became national news, since I was being considered for the role of Christ in a major motion picture. I went to Hollywood for the best Christian reason, which turned into a journey independent of God. Like others who have heard the call of the Master, our "paths of righteousness" are not always in a straight line but often are detoured into the far-off city, like the prodigal of old. By

God's grace, I found my appointed niche in the kingdom of God and not on a Hollywood sound stage.

While attending Tennessee Temple University, my first student pastorate was a shabby wooden one-room chapel on Sunday. On Monday, it reverted to being the town schoolhouse. My pulpit was portable, of course. But to a student in his first parish assignment, this unprepossessing church had all the splendor of a cathedral. As a plain woman might, the building became beautiful when loved. For I was in love with my vision—to serve God and to be a pastor.

At Temple, I portrayed Scrooge in *A Christmas Carol* and did soliloquies of the Danish prince, Hamlet. This was my favorite world—a level of make-believe that would never subside but bring me much emotional pain and heartache until I learned to use it for God. "For I know the thoughts that I think toward you, says the Lord, thoughts of peace and not of evil, to give you a future and a hope" (Jeremiah 29:11).

When my Hollywood plans were settled, I was visited by the inevitable reporters and was deluged by personal mail of different opinions. One writer warned, "If God has called you to be a minister, do not stoop to become a movie star." This statement seemed silly, yet it haunted me.

The professional cinema world opened before me, and I entered it. I was introduced to Hollywood society by the late Henry Wilson, a well-known agent responsible for the discovery of many major talents. Once inside, my priorities shifted. I didn't play the part of Jesus, as I had expected—and which, to my mind, would have made my acting a ministry. Due to many complications, *The Greatest Story Ever Told* was never filmed at 20th Century-Fox. The president of Paramount Pictures, Y. Frank Freeman, felt I could be a potential talent and handed me a Tyrone Power script to memorize for an audition. My focus began changing.

As I found myself thrust into Hollywood society, I began deteriorating spiritually. Hollywood did not guarantee its pilgrims sudden success. To save money, I took a room on a street called Hope in a city called

"The City of Angels." There wasn't much glamour on Hope Street, but it was the beginning of a renewed inner hunger to honor my calling as an ambassador of the Lord God, Christ.

With a sense of desperation, I wrote to Dr. Lee Roberson, president of Tennessee Temple University (now chancellor), about my desire to leave Hollywood and my availability for speaking engagements. That great man of faith understood completely. He didn't need to hear any repentance or any soiled testimony; he had been praying for the fugitive to return and be reinstated.

Through Dr. Roberson's influence and compassion, the New England Fellowship of Evangelicals arranged an autumn New England speaking tour. With a feeling of purpose instead of resignation, I said goodbye to Hollywood.

During the course of my tour, I was dazzled by God's goodness. I found myself in Gardner, and eventually, He opened a glorious and almost miraculous door—I became the pastor of a small church on Mission Street in desperate need of repair. To me, it looked as beautiful as St. Paul's Cathedral in England! For thirty-five years, it was my joy to proclaim the unsearchable riches of God's Word. For almost thirty of those years, we broadcast live in our tri-state area to a potential audience of fifty thousand.

From Hope Street in Hollywood to Mission Street in Gardner was an unforgettable journey! Through it all, I learned the most significant fact of my life. No matter how far a man may go from God, the Father is always waiting with open arms to welcome him back.

For almost four decades, my stage has been pulpit-sized. From it, I have discovered meaning, purpose, and fulfillment.

To God be the glory,

R. Gary Heikkila, PhD

Christos Kurios

Foreword

W. A. Criswell

For a good many years (beyond half a century), I have been a pastor. In those decades I have met hundreds and hundreds of young men in the employ of the church and in the many-faceted ministries of our Lord. If you have ever seen or have ever known Gary Heikkila, you will understand what I mean when I say he is absolutely and truly one of the most gifted and one of the most unusual young preachers and pastors anyone could ever meet in this modern generation.

You will love reading this story. It is one in which all of us have, in past, passed through. You will identify with the young man, Gary. You will weep with him in his sadness. You will feel for him in his despair. You will rejoice with him in his dedication to the Lord. And you will praise God with him in the beautiful ministry he now has in New England.

May God bless the eyes that read these words, and may God no less bring a special blessing to the many people who will follow this story through these exciting and heartwarming pages.

Chapter 1

The Seminarian Goes to Hollywood

THE BUS ROLLED CAREFULLY OUT into the bright sunlight of early morning. Tall and well-built, the young man found himself a seat near the center of the bus as it was leaving the Chattanooga, Tennessee Greyhound station. Newly ordained, Reverend Russell Gary Heikkila leaned eagerly toward the window. He was beginning the first part of his long journey to movie stardom in faraway Hollywood.

Gary, as he preferred to be called, was being considered to play the leading part in a forthcoming major motion picture, *The Greatest Story Ever Told.* It was being produced by Twentieth Century-Fox Studios, and he had been contacted by important people in Hollywood about playing the lead part of Jesus Christ. He was not letting distance deter him.

Having finished his senior year at the Tennessee Temple Schools in Chattanooga (now University) and duly ordained a minister on May 25, 1956, he was now, on May 29, 1957, one year later, cramming himself into a bus seat for a long ride across the continent to the most glamorous city in the entire world, Los Angeles. There he would find Hollywood glittering under the dazzling sun, gleaming in the dark of night, awaiting his imminent arrival.

Of course, he was aware he would be required to change buses several times before he got there, but what were a few discomforts along the way to making a dream come true? This was a dream he had dreamed long ago, and now it was about to become a reality.

He settled back into the seat, which he had to himself, hoping his new suit would not look too lived-in by the time of his arrival. It would take a beating, he knew, and it was the only one he had. Monica, dear Monica, had bought it for him, and furthermore had loaned him $400 in cash to see him through in Hollywood until he became a star.

He had already been practically chosen for the part, and he had with him the letters from Walter Lang at Twentieth Century-Fox, who would be directing the forthcoming picture. Mr. Lang had invited him to come to Hollywood for a test. They were hoping to find an unknown to play the part of Jesus.

Who was more unknown than he? And who could be better for the part than a real minister? Of course, he hadn't actually gotten the part yet, but certainly no one else had a better chance. After seeing Gary's pictures and learning his description—young, over six feet tall, with brown hair and blue eyes--Christ was often pictured as blue eyed and even blond, so that was no problem. The director, Walter Lang, was very impressed with what he saw. Christ was often pictured as blue-eyed and even blond, so that was no problem. Gary felt very confident of getting the part and settled down now in his bus seat, excited to be on his way to fame and fortune.

Monica Evans, his friend, was fully expecting to see him next on the big screen at the Bijou in Chattanooga, playing the part of Christ in this wonderful new religious picture. And she would, he promised himself.

He leaned back, noticing the bus was fairly full, and felt quite lucky to have obtained a whole seat for himself. Becoming more comfortable, he assured himself there was every reason to expect to get the part. Of course, from then on, he need not worry. This whole thing, he reflected, was like a coincidence and was at least a little strange. It had to be fate. Well, maybe not so much fate as perhaps God's will.

The notice had been in the paper almost a year ago at the end of his senior year in the Tennessee Temple Bible School, where he had been studying for the ministry ever since mustering out of the Army in 1954. He had decided while stationed in Korea during his two years of service that he wanted to become an ordained minister, and he had. He had finished his senior year and been ordained at about the time the announcement concerning the coming new picture was seen in the paper.

Louella Parsons, the well-known Hollywood columnist, had mentioned in one of her articles that Twentieth Century-Fox was casting for the role of Jesus in *The Greatest Story Ever Told,* and moreover, the studio was looking for an unknown to play the part. Gary had immediately felt compelled to act upon this item, which he had discovered by accident, and was greatly encouraged by others who enthusiastically told him he was perfect for the part.

Handsome and poised at twenty-four, he had been exposed to the public almost all his life and had no qualms about his appearance, voice, or diction. He had started out very young in the entertainment field—in the eighth grade in school, in fact. At that time, he had conducted his own radio show, called "Songs by Russ," on a local radio station in the small Michigan town of Calumet, where he had grown up.

Since his first name was Russell, he had used that, but it was a name he disliked. Later, he adopted his middle name of Gary. But at that time, everyone had called him Russell or Russ, and his show had been a great success. He was well-liked and sang all of the latest popular songs, continuing his show through nearly the entire eighth grade in school. But tragedy struck suddenly one day, and his career abruptly ended when his voice would no longer do what he wanted it to do. He remembered he was about thirteen at the time. He had stopped singing in his high soprano voice then, turned to talking, and became a radio disc jockey.

All through his high school years, he had conducted a disc jockey show. Also, at about this time, he had become interested in public speaking and was thrilled with his first experience at swaying an audience.

His interests included high school dramatics, and he could well understand and respond to what July Garland had once spoken of as "having a love affair with the audience." He knew that feeling perfectly. It was very satisfying, and he lived for it. His world, he knew, lay somewhere in public life.

Later, he connected his acting ability, his being a complete extrovert, and his desire to spread the Word of God as synonymous in his success in life. He felt that to some degree, a minister must be something of an actor—at least; he must use some of the tools of the acting profession in order to be a truly successful minister. He believed that by dramatizing events in the Bible, they could be made more interesting and would become more real to many who might not otherwise react at all. And he had no doubt of the effectiveness of dramatic experience with the ministry. He had seen the response of those who demonstrated this, had felt it himself, and knew that people responded to it.

He had tried out his ability for dramatic presentation, and while he had not yet applied it to stories taken from the Bible, he had produced and acted in Dickens's *A Christmas Carol* at the Temple Schools with the permission of the president, Dr. Lee Roberson, who was also pastor of the Highland Park Baptist Church in Chattanooga. This play had proven so successful that it had been repeated the following Christmas.

So why should he not have his head in the clouds after the possibility of getting the lead part in this wonderful new religious picture coming up in Hollywood? They were looking for an unknown actor to play the part of Christ; he was somewhat of an actor and thoroughly unknown. And he would certainly understand the part and portray it sincerely. It was undoubtedly God's will, he was convinced. He felt more relaxed while the bus was whisking him away to Hollywood.

What a strange way God has of working out his will, he thought as the scenery flashed by while he was going back over his life, which had brought him from an unremarkable childhood to radio experience and now to this unusual opportunity to become a part of the fantastic world of Hollywood. This world was populated by wonderful people of marvelous capabilities—a world he had long dreamed of.

He began to let his mind wander and could see himself, pragmatically brought up in Northern Michigan, which had a character and climate reminiscent of his family's native Finland. There, in the small town of

Calumet, his people had sought to preserve as much as possible of their native land in the food and even in the traveling, which was done by sleigh, skis, or skates in winter, as in the old country.

Thinking of it brought back to his mind a story he had heard his mother tell in which she said that angels surely watch over children. She had been relating an incident that had happened when he was only three years old. They were on a sleigh ride out in the farm country, and the whole family—including his only sibling, Janice, a sister younger than he—was all bundled up warmly in blankets. The old-fashioned sleigh was being pulled by two huge farm horses, with Grandpa Heikkila holding the reins. As his mother remembered it, the sleigh runner had struck a rock along the way and spilled them all out in every direction as it turned over on the rutted, snowy road. No one was hurt, and they were about to get underway again when his mother discovered that little Russell Gary was missing. At her screaming, everyone jumped out of the sleigh and began looking for him. He was found buried in the deep snow, exactly under the horses' feet. He would have been killed or badly injured had the team begun to pull the sleigh, and Gary believed with his mother that God had surely saved him and that angels were watching over him.

He had also been saved another time, he recalled now as the bus rumbled along—when he was seven. It really had been his own fault. He smiled to himself, remembering this incident. He had been showing off, trying to impress some of his peers with his aquatic prowess, which was not considerable at that time. And in his efforts, he had ostentatiously jumped off the edge of the pool into the water and then found to his dismay he could not touch bottom. His jump had been from the wrong end of the pool with thirteen feet of water under him.

Splashing and gasping and truly drowning while his observers paid him the compliment of believing him when he had said he could swim, he was going under for the third time, splashing and trying to scream with his mouth full of water, when suddenly, he felt strong hands help him through the water to the side of the pool. He gasped for breath, desperately clutching the side of the pool, and looked around to thank the lifeguard who had helped him. There was no one near him. All three lifeguards were sitting in their respective chairs, paying no attention.

A year later, when he was eight, he remembered another time when his life was miraculously saved. He had been staying with his maternal grandparents in the little village of Trimountain, near Calumet. The village was reached by a picturesque winding road that cut through low hills covered with virgin forests. These hills contained copper, and the little community thrived on mining at that time. It was said, he remembered, that anyone who had ever lived in Trimountain would forever have an irresistible urge to return. In winter, the roads were always icy, which suited the natives. They preferred to skate rather than drive cars or sleighs, and they traveled almost everywhere on skates.

It was Valentine's Day, Gary remembered. He could see himself in his mind's eye as he set off on his skates to join his friends at the town skating rink, a journey he took daily.

There were very few cars in Trimountain, but all would skid on the icy roads, and as he swiftly rounded a sharp curve, he felt helpless terror grip him. A skidding car was before him, and it was too late to maneuver on his skates out of its path. There had been no way to escape the car that came skidding toward him, and they crashed full into each other. Vaguely, he remembered the panicky activity around him as they carried him into the emergency room at the Trimountain hospital. And now he felt the panic again he had felt when he had begun screaming, "Where are my legs? Where are my legs?"

His grandfather, Carlson, who was the night watchman at the hospital, had rushed in while Gary was being prepared to go upstairs to the operating room for surgery. His grandfather had excitedly called home and told Gary's grandmother that Gary had been hit by a car, was in the hospital, and had just gone up.

Grandmother Carlson, in her excitement, understood only that poor Gary had been hit by a car and had "gone up"—a gentle colloquial way of saying "gone up to heaven." Their grief was so great until the story was righted that they had rejoiced to find he had sustained a compound fracture of the right leg, which would heal. And heal it did, Gary remembered, though it had always given him some trouble.

"Angels again," Gary muttered to himself as he squirmed in his bus seat and then realized he hadn't been very concerned with angels at that time. In fact, religion had made little impression upon him as he was growing up. His parents had always insisted upon church and Sunday school for his sister, Janice, and himself, and he was baptized and confirmed, but nothing had happened to him inwardly until the war.

Up until the time when he was drafted in 1952, while the fighting was heavy in Korea, he had not been very aware of the war, and he was not possessed of any real religious convictions. He was a Christian and believed in Christ but did not have any deep or personal feelings about it. But when he was drafted and assigned to Company A of the 81st Medium Tank Battalion, he was sent away immediately to take his basic training at Fort Smith, Arkansas. And now he moved in his seat again and tried to stretch his legs as he vividly remembered meeting Chaplain Jack Cutberth there.

The chaplain was a young man in his early thirties, trim, medium height, with dark hair and eyes, and deeply committed to his calling as well as to the military. He had left a profound impression on Gary pertaining to the ministry. He believed in complete immersion and had baptized Gary at the First Baptist Church at Fort Smith, Arkansas in 1952. Gary's life had changed drastically at that time.

Jack was an earnest young man who poured his life into the recruits and had overwhelmed Gary by his dedication to duty and total commitment to Jesus. Cutberth's parents lived at Fort Smith, too, and often entertained "our soldier boys," as they called them. They were gentle, sensitive people and made everyone welcome in their home. He had never met finer people, and Gary soon grew to have great affection and admiration for them as well as for the chaplain.

Gary smiled now, remembering how Jack had taken him to the First Baptist Church at Fort Smith, where he had had a truly wonderful experience of dedicating his life to Christ. He could still feel it—the compelling, all-fulfilling sensation when the knowledge had come over him that he was doing the right thing and that everything in his life was going to come out all right. That feeling, he realized, had left him not weakened, and he thought with a thrill of what it was not leading him to. He looked around at the people on the bus with him. He was certain that not a single one of them was going to Hollywood to fulfill a dream, as he was. He felt very fortunate and thanked his Lord Jesus, knowing Jesus would see him through. The bus made a stop and then proceeded on, and Gary continued to reminisce as they wheeled swiftly along the highway going west.

His thoughts went back to Chaplain Cutberth and the training they had undergone in preparation for being shipped out overseas. He had grumbled with the rest of the raw recruits, and like them, had felt sore and tired. As they trained, he had found that the commander had a grim sense of humor, which could make them remember they were not just playing war games but were being prepared to fight in vicious combat in a mortal conflict. He had reminded them quite forcibly that it behooved them to take it seriously, since they would not all come back.

As they were crawling along on the ground under live machine gun fire in their field training, he recalled the commander saying casually, "Keep your heads down, boys. I'd rather not have anyone killed today." This must have jolted others, as it had him, into realizing that while these were not real bullets, it would be very different in actual battle.

Their commander had also warned them just as casually about the rattlesnakes that seemed to own most of the land there in rural Arkansas and suggested dourly that if they encountered a rattlesnake and machine gun fire at the same time to choose the snake.

Gary smiled now, remembering this, and then he noticed a small girl in front of him who had turned around and was smiling at him over the back of her seat.

"Where you goin'?" she asked.

Gary, taken by surprise, replied, "To Hollywood."

"Are you a movie star?" she asked with appropriate awe.

"Not yet. But I hope to be," he admitted spontaneously, smiling.

The little girl turned around and said loudly to the lady with her, "That man's a movie star. He's in the movies."

"Really?" the older woman asked, turning to beam at him. By that time, the entire bus was buzzing, and the people were craning their necks to look at the "movie star on their bus.

"Oh, would you give me your autograph?" an elderly across the aisle from him asked, shoving a tiny notebook at him.

He gravely signed his name, "Gary Heikkila," and when the bus stopped soon after, the deluge came.

He could hardly get a sandwich eaten between signing his name and smiling back at those who had not even glanced his way before but were now whispering behind hands held carefully and ogling him.

"Isn't he handsome?" one woman said loudly enough to be heard several seats away. "I just knew he was somebody. He's going to be Jesus in "*The Greatest Story Ever Told!*"

"When's it coming?" her seatmate asked excitedly.

"Oh, I don't know. Soon, I guess, but I'll look for him. He'll be the main one. He looks like Jesus, doesn't he?" she asked, and added, "If he had a beard," daring to turn her head and take a quick glance at him, almost fearfully.

And now Gary felt like Jesus, wanting to bless all these dear people who had no idea how good an actor he really was or how realistically he would play the part of Jesus but were giving him credit anyway. He wanted to bless them, because he felt that he knew Jesus. And he felt divinely chosen to play this part as no one else could play it, and these people were already accepting him.

He tried to sleep that first night on the bus but found the hours long in his cramped position and soon drifted back to remembering his not-so-distant war days and the ship that had carried them away to the Korean conflict zone. He had spent a short time with his parents first, and then—off to war.

It had been a lark to the boys, and to hear them, one could have taken their troop ship for a pleasure cruise. The talk was all about the girls they were leaving behind, with jokes and smart talk and nothing morbid mentioned, such as not all of them coming back or some coming back maimed. They looked forward to the girls they would meet and the fun they would have. There was a myriad of dirty jokes, practical jokes, and rough language mixed with careless laughter, but underneath it all, Gary had been aware that they all felt the same—so scared they could cry, but they never would.

Then, as the ship moved out over the endless water, the vastness and aloneness had brought them more serious thoughts, and emotions rose high. To Gary, it had seemed that the Pacific Ocean was divided into zones—here, they thought about girls; a little further on, it was their homes and families; still closer to Korea, it they talked about their training; and finally, they discussed how they would die. Would it be a sudden bullet? A flame-thrower? A mine? Which way was the worst? They discussed the pros and cons and became absorbed in heated arguments that covered a fear they could not face.

Then came a day when the sea was as smooth as glass. Gary remembered standing at the rail, thinking about the Lord's walk on the water. He could almost see Jesus on that smooth surface. *It would hardly seem a miracle on a sea like that,* he had thought. But he was soon roused form his reverie by a lifeboat drill—an exercise so serious, sobering, and hazardous to that group of youthful inexperienced warriors that everything else was forgotten. The party was over. Enemy submarines were suspected, and they all knew their ship could be blasted out of the water at any moment of the day or night. It was chilling knowledge that fundamentally changed their outlook on life forever.

He shivered now on the bus and pulled his coat tighter around him, since the night had grown cold. He stretched out a little on the double seat, hoping he could get some sleep before morning and wishing he had not remembered that experience. But his mind buzzed on, and he could see the ship and feel the tension that had engulfed them all. Friendships had been galvanized aboard that ship. A friend might save your life, or you might save his. Friendships grew fast and deep, while the ship plowed perilously on through mined waters. Then they had stopped briefly at Japan.

They had seen their storied mountains, and he remembered them now as if he were still looking at them. He could still feel the charming atmosphere of the Orient. He pulled his long legs up into the double seat and tried to sleep, but his mind tumbled on and carried him along.

After a briefing in Japan, all their minds had been mostly on the fearsome work ahead. And finally, they had come to Inchon Harbor in South Korea. Here they had really felt fear. The harbor was mined, with only submarine nets protecting their vessels at anchor, giving them the helpless feeling of little ants surrounded by potential destruction.

It had been extremely frustrating to have to depend entirely upon the ship's crew to get them through while they were forced to wait helplessly at the railings. Listening to the heavy guns in the distance had made them itch to grab a gun and start shooting at something—anything—to defend themselves. They all felt the dreadful tension. But all this was routine for the processors at Inchon. The new arrivals were checked off one by one on clipboards and herded here and there by cold-eyed officers who carefully avoided any personal contact. Then finally, they had been shepherded onto a train for Pusan. Pusan—ah, he remembered Pusan. He would never forget that city.

Pusan was like nothing on earth he had ever seen or dreamed of. They had been too late to see it in its quiet beauty, as it had been before the war for so many peaceful years. Life there had been spent in tranquil, stylized living. The women were lovely, docile, and obedient, clinging to a way of life that gave them a delicate, refined beauty—refined mainly, perhaps, by suffering. But the strength of their faith in their way of achieving happiness was stronger than any enemy they could ever erase, hard as they tried. It was so wrong to disturb these peaceful, gentle, quiescent people.

The men seemed shorter than American men, and the women were slender and delicate-looking, but the burdens they carried and the suffering they endured belied the seeming weakness of their delicate forms. They showed no emotion but sweetness and calm, no matter what pain they endured. The men, as ceremonial as the women, displayed no coarse-featured passion and seemed as calm in their souls as in their countenance. They were a peaceful people. They had no god of war.

Many gods they had, but all were peaceful gods. Happiness was their goal, and contentment was their way. The ugly, violent passions had been subdued long, long ago, and they lived serenely in peace and harmony with lovely gardens, homes, schools, and places of worship formed so beautifully that they seemed but a part of nature. Gary had read of this beautiful country, knowing they would come here, but he was not prepared for the ravages of a savage war that had torn it to pieces before they arrived.

He stirred unhappily in his uncomfortable, cold bus seat, hearing the breathing, snoring, sighing busload of people trying to get through a night amidst the whining of the engine, jostling over the rough pavement, and smells of exhaust that offended the nostrils and dried the throat.

When will the night end? Gary wondered. Then he settled into a more comfortable position, still thanking God he had a full seat to stretch out at least a little in. His thoughts wandered back to the shocking sight of that once lovely and now pitiful city of Pusan. It had been a fine city of light industry, chemicals, and textiles, including the beautiful cloth from which they made their clothing. It had been built in beauty, symbolism, peace, quiet, and contentment over a long period of time.

But now the home of a million souls was being brutally torn apart by war. It was a shambles, and Gary had thought when he had seen this once happy city that the most miserable place to be in any war must be halfway between the battle lines and the safe zone in the rear. If you were all the way up at the front, then survival was the motive of your life, with no dull moments and no time to meditate on the horrors. But in between, where you could hear the artillery and where it was perfectly possible for the enemy to come marching right down the street in front of your door, was where the real fear was—the real misery, the real terror, the real horror of war. And these people, he knew, had been forced to live with this for a long, long time.

He moved restlessly, forgetting again his own minor discomfort as he thought of the ghastly futility of this gruesome war, as all wars have always been merely an excuse for exhibiting the brutalities still remaining in man after all these many ages. *What must have been man's beginning, to make these callous ferocities so hard to shed?* Gary wondered as he tried to sleep on that first endless night on the rumbling bus.

Chapter 2

Reflections on War in Korea

Gary's mind went back to the war days in spite of his efforts to think of other things. Those impressions were too strong to be pushed back once the floodgates of memory had been opened.

He remembered the landing of the troops in Pusan and the shock of seeing a city held in a vise of terror. His own duties had been not on the battlefield, but to his discontent, were backstage in the mailroom at Pusan. He remembered his chagrin. This mundane task galled; he had been prepared to do battle to free those pitiful, blameless people from their yoke of fear. Instead, he must stay behind walls and sort mail.

He realized that his disgust had shown itself at least enough to merit a stiff lecture by his superior officer—ending, he remembered, in being very bluntly and soberly reminded, "The mail is our lifeline, Heikkila." He had become more acquiescent, if not content, and he had handled the mail with dispatch and conscience from then on and all during that period of time. But he had been determined, he remembered now, scrunching himself into the cold, hard bus seat, that he would not be long relegated to mailman if he could help it. And he remembered how he had found the way to compensate for his humble and obscure position by using his talent for the ministry, which had been developed back in the Fort Smith boot camp by the indefatigable Chaplain Jack Cutberth.

Gary was determined that if he could not join the fighting forces, he would not be content with merely handling mail. And since he had much free time, he decided he would make use of it to further his ministry of Christ's message whenever possible. He had been issued a license to preach by the Baptist church in Fort Smith, and he would be a chaplain and spread the Word as best he could. This decision had given his life new impetus, and he had begun to make plans.

His earlier estimation of the men of God had, however, undergone quite a change in his line of duty as a serviceman. The first chaplain he had encountered back in boot camp, Chaplain Cutberth, had been truly unique, he now realized. He had not since then met one who was even remotely like him. Those he had met since, on the ship and on the battlefield, were a totally different breed of men and were even vastly different from each other.

He smiled, remembering, twisting to get his feet up, that there had been one thing they all had in common; they were men—but what a variety of men. Some were deeply committed to God and their fellowmen; others seemed to be totally oblivious to the spiritual qualities. Others had serious drinking problems, and some were so imbued with fundamentalism that they were badly misplaced as chaplains on a battlefield, where the need was to kill or be killed.

But now he remembered with pleasure the first answer to his constant prayers for duty as a chaplain's assistant. This had come about fairly soon after he had begun to be a mailman. He had the right to expect this opportunity—or any other opportunity that should arise, he reminded himself—because it was on his record that he had worked with the chaplain at Fort Smith, and he had also been the ship's chaplain for a time. Therefore, he was not totally inexperienced. And as the Lord would have it, shortly after he made his wishes to be an assistant chaplain known to the commanding officer, an opening had suddenly developed for him.

He remembered his excitement and his awe that the Lord had responded so quickly to his prayers. It had come about as they were all gathered in Pusan for a big Christmas Eve service. They had organized quite a celebration by acquiring from among their ranks a fine organist, and they had even made a crèche.

All of the top brass, including the post commander, had turned out. The carols had been rehearsed to perfection and the candles lit. All was in readiness, but the chaplain was not there. No one knew where he was.

Gary's mind went back to this awful calamity, feeling again the surprise and horror of the moment, thankful it was past. But he also felt again the deep concern, the agitation, the empty feeling of anguish he had felt for that one helpless moment when he had gone down to the chaplain's quarters and found him completely drunk. That had been devastating. There would be no Christmas sermon, no celebration, no wonderful Christmas Eve to celebrate the marvelous birth of Christ. He felt again the desolation he had felt at that moment and moaned as he turned in his seat to get some sure ease from both physical and mental anguish.

And then he remembered, as he had stood looking down at the booze-sodden chaplain lying in a rumpled bunk, his own aroused determination. There had been no time to ask permission. He had to take the bull by the horns; he had to act. And act he had. He smiled now, feeling more warm and comfortable than he had all night. He had come through in a crisis.

He could see himself now, trembling a little, but bravely putting on the drunken chaplain's stole, resolving to put his untried license to preach to the test. He had gone upstairs then, wearing the chaplain's stole, and was greeted with applause by the audience, whose members were not yet aware that he was not the chaplain.

Resolutely, he marched up to the center of the stage before the now hushed audience members, who had just begun to grasp that this was not their chaplain. In a somewhat shaking voice but with what he hoped was a commanding appearance, he made the announcement. "The chaplain is ill," he began. And then, as he spoke, the resonance of his voice gave him courage, and he said, "I will deliver the message."

Silence met this. But it had not deterred him. He took a step aside to the podium on which the chaplain's large Bible already rested, inadvertently open to Isaiah 5:2, which speaks of "Woe to them … whom wine inflame," and he began with verse 22, which again says, "Woe to them that are mighty to drink wine and men of strength to mingle strong drink."

It had seemed to be a direct message for his sermon, and he had made full use of it. He, a Pfc, facing his commander, trembling a little, had declaimed mightily on the devils of drink. And they had listened. They listened to him. He had felt it—sensed it. And at that time, something had happened to him, something very important. He had heard at that moment the call from the Lord. He had heard it and felt it clearly. It was a clear and distinct call, and he had known then, on that stage, on that Christmas Eve, the truth. He was going to be a minister.

He had known it, accepted it, and thanked God for the call, all the while standing before that hushed and listening audience, knowing the message from his heart was being felt by them and that with their acceptance had come the really wonderful acceptance of God. He had been truly ordained in a more heavenly way than he had ever dreamed of, and he knew that he would never turn away.

And he still knew it now, he told himself on his way to Hollywood, where the Lord might not sway, but where he would pave the way. He would bring God forth amidst the most evil of all places. It was a place of make-believe and false values, he had heard, where any church was dwarfed by the buildings of movieland sets, and the production stages were filled with unclothed female flesh cavorting for the entertainment of the lascivious in this most ungodly of worlds.

But here, he believed, was the most fertile soil of all for a minister to tread. Here, he truly felt, was needed the knowledge of the Redeemer, more than in any other place on earth. And perhaps he was the only one on earth who could dare to do this and who would persevere until he had brought the glorious name of Christ before this lost world. He would help the whole world to see the goodness of the Lord as He really was. And from where, possibly, could he better reach the whole world than from Hollywood as a beloved and famous movie star?

Who in all the world could play the part of Jesus Christ, our Lord, more truly than a real man of God? Certainly his work was cut out for him, Gary assured himself as he twisted in the uncomfortable bus seat, enduring much discomfort in the long reaches of the night. Hollywood was a land to which the Bible verse of Isaiah 5: 20, was surely speaking: "Woe unto them that call evil good, and good, evil; that put darkness for light, and light for darkness; that put bitter for sweet, and sweet for bitter."

This was Hollywood. He had heard of the iniquities there. And it, of the entire world, needed saving. How better to save it than by the enlightened playing of the character of Christ by a truly religious man? The player of this part should be a believer—a true lover of Christ who could also act. This would lend the real drama needed for this important picture based upon the life of Christ. He could make Christ real to so many people. What a wonderful opportunity. He alone in the entire world could most sincerely and best play this part. He thrilled with the thought.

He, among all other actors, could most sincerely portray the goodness, holiness, beauty, kindness, and true love that Christ had for mankind. He could bring it to the world for Christ. It was in his own heart, and he trembled with the knowledge. He felt what Christ must have felt—the forgiveness and readiness to sacrifice Himself for all humanity. He had given His own life to save the world, to have their sins forgiven and their souls saved for a glorious afterlife with Him. For this, Christ had worn the crown of thorns and let Himself be crucified. Gary could understand Christ now as never before—truly, deeply understand Him.

No matter what the sacrifice to himself might be, Gary was willing to suffer as Jesus had suffered, if necessary, to bring the light of Jesus to the world. He would never have a better opportunity than this, he told himself. A picture was being made for the purpose of depicting the life of Christ and His sacrifice, and Gary was born to play the part. It was a rapturous moment for Gary, and he forgot where he was. It filled his soul with glory that faded away but slowly.

His legs began to ache, and he was parched and miserable as he turned and twisted to get some rest. He could not remember a night being so long. But his mind, stirred as it was by his earnest purpose, feeling truly some of the suffering that physical pain brought, was now turning back to that miserable waste in the once beautiful city of Pusan during the war.

He could see himself as he was then, having been made an interim chaplain during the wait after Christmas for the new replacement chaplain to arrive. It had filled his soul with wonder to have become so suddenly, even for this short interim, a chaplain on the base there. He had taken his duties seriously and filled in the gaps between the leaving and incoming chaplains—which were several—as best he could. He had thanked God for thus moving his ministry so fast, faster than he had expected, and he was determined to do his best. He had seen, too, that there was really a great need for preaching to be done in Korea. He sighed, remembering sadly.

In an orphanage near Pusan, he had found half-dead babies fathered by American troops; he had held one in his arms who had been abandoned by the roadside. The girl was so weak from lack of food that the baby could not hold her head up. He had cried then, and he wept now in his heart as he remembered that deep sorrow. And all those babies had not come from women who were acquiescent to the foreign soldiers, either. Most were not.

But who talks about those particular atrocities of war? he thought with bitterness. The American public, shielded as it has been, was not even aware of the rapes committed by their own sons, fathers, husbands, and future husbands in the field of battle. But the wake of fatherless American-fathered babies left in war-torn countries told the tale, he knew.

When we, the public, say atrocities, he thought now in the darkness of the night, *we mean the torture of weaponry wounds and gashes and slow death. But what of the wounds of the spirits of those beautiful, innocent women and even very young girls in being molested and raped and left to bear the shame of a child not wanted, a marriage prevented or broken—a shame that thrusts them irrevocably out of home and any happiness ever? What of the mothers of children already born to them—mothers torn from family and loved ones because of being violated, forced by brute strength to have a bastard child whom all the world can see is of mixed blood and is never to be accepted?*

Boldly, the perpetrators of these atrocities say, "This is war. And war means violation of women as well as bloodshed. It has always been so." And so it has. And evidence makes it apparent that it still is today. *While the American public proudly and foolishly pretends otherwise,* Gary admitted with shame for his fellow men.

"Oh," we say, "these are the little sins of war, not to be noticed." And so they are easily forgotten when the fighting is over and our boys come marching home, Gary thought cynically. But what about the babies of our boys who were dying or being nursed back to health in that orphanage, which was filled to overflowing with these mixed-blood, bastard children they left behind? So many thousands of them. What kind of life would they have? Bastards or mixed blood are never accepted—not in our own society, and certainly not in societies as old as this, where family ties are everything and virginity is a requirement of marriage. Bastard children are repulsed, and the mother is castigated, whether married or not. And where a wife is little more than chattel and can be replaced by a man's desire, she has no defense whatever. And these women definitely do not give themselves to men freely. They are, in the majority, forced, Gary knew, sorrowfully, from his contacts with the perpetrators.

And what of the children bereft of mothers—of the future husband robbed of his most precious possession, a virgin bride, by whom he and he alone may have children? And what of the young girl, unmarried, unmarriageable now in a hostile society, who must care for and raise an unwanted child by herself with no adequate way to do it? What of the violated wife forced from home and children? What of the children, deprived of a family, of having two parents, of having even the barest necessities of life—what of them? *Did any man with intent to rape ever stop to think of what he was doing to the society he violated along with the body of a young girl, wife, or mother?* Gary wondered and then decided it was doubtful.

Korea's society was old. It was stylized, immutable, and unchanging, and there was no place in it for the wholesale molestation of women. Even those who the American public kidded themselves were civilized American soldiers had violated just as many Korean women, Gary knew, as any uncivilized army ever had. The only effect of civilization at all upon them was that they did not kill, maim, or mutilate the women quite as brutally. But the impregnated all they could and laughed about it.

Gary turned again in his cold bus seat, tortured by this awful knowledge that had been pushed upon him as chaplain and wishing now he did not have to know it. But knowledge cannot be reversed. And while no one talked about these small sins, he knew they loomed as large as murder to those whose bodies had been violated. These violations were still shockingly and shamefully evident in the violated and devastated country, he also knew, and they could not be denied. Pusan was teeming with pitiful bastard children of American fathers, as were all the war-torn areas overseas. Gary twisted in an agony of shame for his kind—for humanity.

He remembered now the Jeep trips he had taken when, because of his interim chaplainship, he found himself the only Pfc in Korea with his own Jeep and driver. This had made it possible for him to go out among the Koreans as well as among his own troops.

People comfortably at home in America would really experience a rude awakening, he thought, if those who made the thrilling movies, filling the theaters to which people avidly flocked, would point their cameras at the faces of people in the villages and cities that were ruined instead of the Hollywood-made foxholes. Those concocted foxholes showed only the glories of war, reflected in the faces of made-up men who, in making-believe battles, "did-or died" and then afterward went cheerfully out to lunch. But the reality of war was so very different.

Admittedly, war was tough on the front lines and on soldiers in combat, but a look at the civilians suffering around them would make pacifists of all humanity, if they could really see it. Such suffering far surpassed all the blood, guts, and gore of men who were wounded or died in battle. Civilian suffering was more like the suffering of those who were wounded and saved but came back minus legs, arms, and parts of bodies, with hands, hearing, sight, or even mobility gone. Then having to live thus the rest of their lives, Gary concluded bitterly to himself, would be the real suffering.

It was like that for civilians, too, who had to live on, their homes destroyed, their land devastated, their families killed and tortured, separated and lost. Hunger, fear for their lost children, and homelessness became a permanent condition with which to live the rest of their lives. What of them? They, too, were shot, shelled, wounded, maimed, crippled, and sickened, and some were violated, both men and women, by beasts in human bodies whose lusts were actually aroused by battle, death, and suffering.

There were friends in human form in every army whose lust must be vented on innocent human beings—innocents like the American public, who never dreamed of such heinous sexual crimes as these. Innocent people were subjected to a war that came unbidden to their land. The American public never knew this horror that many of their own men participated in, and he hoped they never would.

"Oh, but this is war," the perpetrators and their defenders had excused themselves by saying when anyone protested, and Gary cringed in remembering a bold captain who had explained, "War, my boy! War! Where real men are not squeamish." But Gary had been forced to conclude they were not even men, whether real or not, but hyenas who laughed at suffering.

Gary moaned as he squirmed in his seat now and returned to the present, wondering in the night how anyone endured just one seat on a bus when a double seat was so painful. Thank heaven he had this full seat. And why couldn't he sleep? Everyone else seemed to be sleeping. But his mind churned on relentlessly, and he was back again in Korea, going among those whose country they were using for that terrible war. He had sat there beside his Jeep driver in Pusan, looking around as they drove through the torn city, completely stunned.

As he had looked at those gentle people, he could see the strain of fear on every face. Children wandered aimlessly about, understanding nothing, comprehending only that they were somehow lost. Many did not even cry. Their shock was too great. Many had lost one parent—perhaps both. Some had been flatly deserted in the ensuing panic. These children were homeless, naked, cold, starving, dying, eating out of garbage cans or piles of waste in which there was nothing nourishing in all of Pusan, wandering from pile to pile, from dump to dump forever, and slowly starving to death. The adults were in the same condition—homeless, ragged, lost, confused, fearful, ever on guard, and distrustful of all humanity. Not knowing where to turn, they wandered on in aimless horror.

There was no war production going on in Pusan—no production of any kind, no parades, and no politicians posturing before microphones, boasting about their winning the war. There was nothing in Pusan. There was not even enough money for a black market. A city of one million human beings was devastated, violated, and scattered, and its people were left to roam an empty city, broken, torn, and ravaged. And they couldn't leave. How could they? Where could they go? But how could they stay?

While they had to stay, they glared at the American troops with baleful eyes—those "friendly allies" who had come to "help" them. Who could be friendly with such "allies"—these strangers who were tearing their delicately beautiful country to pieces? The lovely winding lanes and the carefully nurtured, beautiful natural flowerbeds of the residential districts had been desecrated by the tanks and explosives of these "allies." And with mines and nets in the harbor, the people could not even get fish for supper.

Starving and uprooted, left to wither and die in the unnourishing streets and waysides, they still had their dreams; Gary had discovered when he could find a way to talk to them. They still had the dreams common to all mankind. When it was ended, they dreamed of going back, of beginning again, of finding lost ones, and even of being happy. Ah, dreams ... that generation would dream in vain.

It had broken his heart, and he still felt the pain. The Koreans had had the same hopes and dreams of all mankind. They hated nobody, and they only wished the war would end. But the war had seemed endless. He remembered becoming restless there and deciding to exercise his chaplain's privileges by taking a Jeep ride outside the city to look at what was left of that gentle countryside.

Chapter 3

More Reflections

Too chilled before dawn to sleep, Gary recalled an incident in Pusan that he would never forget. It had been a beautiful May Day, and he had paid little attention when his driver took an unfamiliar road. Winding their way along a ridge above the harbor, he had suggested they stop and enjoy the view.

Suddenly he realized their Jeep was surrounded by very strange-looking people—people such as he had never seen in his life. They staggered toward the Jeep and surrounded it, seeming to be apparitions and yet very real. Incredibly ragged and covered with bandages, they were obviously in great pain. They staggered and even crawled toward the Jeep in their ghastly deformities as if to engulf it in their tortured misery and drag it down with them. A horror had filled Gary's very soul.

As they came closer, he had seen their terrible deformities. Some had no noses; some mouths were only gaping holes. Most had no teeth. Their eyes were staring, some glaring madly, and others were also even missing limbs. They looked like a mob scene in a horror movie. He had been almost paralyzed, seeing them close up in reality. On they pushed, crowding around the Jeep, moaning, jabbering, gasping, and trying to talk—but of what, he had no idea. His only thought had been to get away from them, for he had suddenly realized with the deepest revulsion that they were lepers.

He did not remember in his surprise and anguish what he knew full well—that no one can catch leprosy. It can be communicated only through long and close association of many years, and then it is not usually contracted, as shown by those who work with lepers. His driver had inadvertently driven them into the leprosarium of a veteran's hospital nearby and was as surprised as he.

At first, Gary had shrunk from these monstrosities and urged his driver to get away quickly, but when they could not more except to run over some of the monstrous people, he begun to feel pity and spoke with some of them.

Many were on crude crutches, and several fell to the ground, apparently from the excitement of seeing people from the outside world. It was evident they were prisoners of the hospital and isolated from all other human beings. They were the most pathetic sight his eyes had ever seen, and he remembered now, with his heart aching at the memory, how pitiful they had been.

The driver was alert to leave when they could, and soon they had driven on, but Gary knew then that try as he might, he would never be able to forget the scene he left behind as they had slowly traveled off on the winding scenic road which he no longer enjoyed. He had not known such misery existed in this world. They had been hideous, waving to them the best they could, dragging themselves along and still waving.

Gary was puzzled over his own reaction, yet as he remembered it, he had suddenly thought of Jesus and how He had cleansed the leper, unafraid. But Gary was afraid that for the life of him, he could not have forced himself to touch one of those pitiful people. He had found at that moment that he could not even pray. It had made him nauseated to look at them; they were so hideous. But they were also helpless. And though he had often longed and prayed for the gift of healing, he felt these people were even beyond that. His reaction had been pure and simple panic at his first glimpse of that horrible disease. And immediately after that had come a deep shame within himself. He had not stood up to the test as he wished he had. Would he ever?

He groaned in his seat on the bus as he turned to throw off this horror, with regret again enveloping him after all these years. He could still see the lepers in his mind's eye, standing there in a motley and unbelievable group, watching the Jeep pull away, while one of the men in the back of the crowd had caught his eye because of his left leg, which had seemed to hang as if by a thread, with the bone entirely eaten through. The leg above the knee was simply dangling, and he had no crutch. But even so, he had wanted so badly to look that he had picked up the flopping leg somehow and hurled himself crablike across the ground on one arm and leg, with his other leg hanging on his arm. He struggled in this manner just to get close enough to simply look at other human beings from the outer world.

Why had that awful image stayed with Gary so clearly? He wondered this now, tensed in agony at the shame of his reaction, which had been horror and pity mixed with a fear so real that he wondered now if it was fear of the disease or of the loneliness he had seen in the eyes of those men in their eagerness to view others. Could it be the loneliness he was afraid of—even more than the disease? Was the loneliness the most awful part of what they suffered? he asked himself. And had the Lord shown him those men to make him realize that no matter how much he had to suffer in this inexplicable life, he would never be as badly off as the man who must carry his leg on his arm? He could not rid himself of the deep sense of shame, as they had driven off.

He wondered about this now and puzzled over the feelings he had experienced. Though pity almost broke his heart, he had wondered at the endurance of man and hoped those men had the consolation of Christ to help them in their bitter suffering. Had they ever been converted? Did they have God's help, or were they strong enough to endure what must be without the loving hand of Christ to guide them, as he was guided in his lesser distress?

He would have liked to help them, but he had realized that this was completely impossible, mainly because he was not yet really an ordained minister but only a chaplain's assistant and because there was simply no way. He had firmly determined then, he recalled, to become an ordained minister, and to do that, he must have proper theological training. He had begun at once to find a school to which his attributes would be acceptable as soon as his military stint was completed. This had turned out to be the Tennessee Temple Schools in Chattanooga, Tennessee. And it had been from there he had boarded this bus, where he was now spending a long and thoughtful (if uncomfortable) first night of several before he would reach his fantastic destination in far-off Hollywood.

He remembered now, clearly, that his entire Korean experience had ended with but one single conversion—the Korean houseboy who had so cheerfully served them all. He had converted Hon to Christianity just before they left.

Hon, the houseboy, had seen chaplains come and go. Just before Gary left Korea, Hon came to him and asked to pray the sinner's prayer to receive Jesus into his heart. The young man wanted to be a true disciple of Jesus Christ. Looking back now, Gary felt he could endure the rest of this long night's sleeplessness and misery, thinking of that proud moment. He had been deeply humbled by Hon's decision; because it made him feel his one single moment of rightness in that entire, awful war. Hon would probably never have become a Christian had he not been there with his message of the Lord. And after that, Gary had been more determined than ever to become a full servant of the Lord by being made an ordained minister of the Baptist church.

His replacement chaplain, he now recalled, had been a corker. He was rough and tough but an evangelical minister who condemned even the mild cussword "heck" and preached sermons about it. He was not a man who was easy to get close to or to understand. He had another personality, it was plain to Gary, that he kept closed off and under strict domination.

Gary, shifting now as the grayfish dawn began to lighten the windows of the rolling bus, thought he could understand that. In fact, he felt a kindred spirit in that way and would have liked to have gotten to know this chaplain better. Gary felt that he, too, had another side of himself that sometimes caused him discomfort. This side took downright willpower to suppress at times when he was tempted, as he sometimes was, to allow this self to rule. But he had kept a tight rein on his own other nature and had been rewarded by the recommendation from his commanding officer, Lt. Col. William Linton. He was very proud of this and could easily recite every word of it by heart.

"CITATION FROM LT. COL. WILLIAM LINTON, COMMANDING OFFICER," he remembered clearly. Then it had said, "I wish to personally commend you for your superior work as Chaplain's assistant during the period 1 March 1953 through 5 January, 1954. Your able leadership, adaptability, and abiding devotion to duty, coupled with your exemplary conduct and behavior, have resulted in material assistance to the religious and moral program of this battalion. Your faithful and loyal service and understanding and cooperative attitude, along with your effectiveness, present a positive contribution to the religious civilities of this command."

This was a most satisfactory statement, and he had easily learned it by heart. He had been admired by some for his unusually retentive memory, which had also been admired during his school years. He had been thankful for this ability more than once in his participation in high school dramatics. It would be a great help now, he realized, in memorizing acting parts.

As the lightening dawn crept further through the windows of the bus, he remembered something that had happened after he was mustered out and leaving Korea; he had fallen into a dreadfully deep depression. It had come upon him unexpectedly as he was departing, and on the ship home, he had been so unhappy that he had to restrain himself at times from throwing himself overboard.

He had wanted to end it all; the suffering of others had gotten to him. He felt a depressing, futile helplessness at going home from that war-torn country, leaving behind those patient, innocent people, devastated, wrested from every faith they held, and leaving nothing to replace it. He felt the emptiness. He wanted to stay and help them, but since this was impossible, he made up his mind to return someday and establish an orphanage for the pitiful homeless and starving children of the streets there. His heart had been torn with nameless grief to be leaving them in their misery and needs.

He determined to make this orphanage his life's work, but first he must return to his own country and obtain a minister's full ordination. Then he would return to Pusan, minister to these people, and help these many innocent suffering children who had no homes and nowhere to go. He would never forget them, he promised himself as the ship had carried him away.

He had not realized the strain of that constant vigilance they had all been under in Korea, and now all of a sudden, upon leaving, he had been overcome with a deep, pervading morbidity. Everything was so futile—so terrible, so senseless. What was the use of anything? Why bother to live in such a world? Truly, he had felt as if he had taken all he could. Even his efforts at prayer had been affected, and he no longer felt the reality of his prayers or his faith.

He had been overwhelmed by the feeling that life was totally helpless. He saw only the utter futility of it all and was not even happy to be going home. Home had no reality for him. He had been keyed up for so long throughout his tour of duty that when the tension ended, his emotions had seemed to burst and collapse like a balloon.

He could feel nothing. And he wondered, if he felt this way, not even having seen any real battle action in Korea, how much more depressed must those feel who had seen it? And now they too, were going home—to what? Was life worth living in such a world? He felt that he was going home to nothing. His life had been rudely interrupted by an ugly interlude that no one had needed. It was all so pointless.

But as the days passed on the ship, his spirits had risen, and so had those of the rest of the troops. They had begun to realize that they were the lucky ones, and from then on, a steadily growing carnival atmosphere had taken hold of them.

They alternated between whooping it up and rehashing their experiences, with each trying to outdo the other in tales of derring-do. But he, Gary remembered, had alternated his whooping it up with the boys with the study of his new government-issue New Testament. He had begun to realize that he had a battle to fight now within himself.

The attack of depression he had experienced had worried him, and he had tried to convince himself that it was due to the unnatural life he had lived for so long. But he knew it really came from his other self, and he knew he would have to battle this other side—this dark side, this willful side of himself—at some time or another, inevitably, before he could turn his life over to the confines of a school of divinity. There he would be made forever into a sedate minister of Christ and forsake all the worldly pleasures that others could so unthinkingly give in to.

He had begun to realize man's nature has two sides, and one side did not want the kind of life he had planned to adopt. He had fought this inner battle alone on the ship, aided only by his prayers, which came hard for a time, and then came gushing forth in supplication, and he had felt his strength growing and the willful side, which was almost as strong as his other side, weakening a little. His battle was long and hard, but by the time the ship had carried him to California, he stepped off and kissed the ground, as did some of the others, because they loved their country, and they had been Korea. And then, somehow, he knew the battle was won, and he was ready for the Temple School of the Bible.

Now he knew he needed just a little more sleep on this bus before the busload of people aroused and he would have to join them. So he closed his eyes again and slept on for an hour till the bus stopped and they had to get off. Breakfast was uppermost in his mind when he followed the sleepy crowd eagerly into the warmth of the busy cafe.

Chapter 4

Reflections on Monica

SOON THEY HAD ALL CROWDED back on the bus, which bore them away over the countryside again with sun in the windows from the east. In after-breakfast contentment, they traveled quietly, and Gary slept for two more hours to make up for lost sleep during his mentally busy night.

When he awoke, he enjoyed the countryside as he watched it pass by from the window. He saw they had passed through Arkansas in the night and were now in Oklahoma. The plains and farms were new to him, and he tried to watch as much as he could, but his eyes closed as he dozed again until noon. After the lunch stop, he wondered how he would make it through the second night, and he knew there were three more to come. Would he ever live through it?

Before long, he found himself deep in thought. The monotonous, flat countryside slid by unnoticed as he withdrew into his inner self and thought of what had brought him to this bus seat, spinning away from what had been his home for three years of divinity school at the Tennessee Temple Schools. The school complex included an elementary school, high school, and college, seminary, and Bible school all on one campus. It was not large, but what it lacked in size, it made up in quality.

His first student pastorate had been at the Stanley Baptist Chapel, one of the many chapels of the enormous Highland Park Baptist Church. He remembered that Professor Louis Hale had always been on the scene whenever he conducted services there. He had also conducted services in the prisons of the Chattanooga area, with Professor Hale always at his side.

Gary, as he was now called—for by the time he had joined the service, he had long been called by his middle name—remembered that his Bible school years had not been confined completely to studies. He was not a boy but a veteran, and he was beginning to understand the loneliness and need of a man for "a helpmeet" who the Lord in his bounty had promised. And now Gary remembered his awareness in the instance of his first love, Monica. *Monica Evans, the dearest, sweetest girl on earth,* he thought now as the bus bore him swiftly away from her.

Monica, dear Monica. Here he was, on this bus, wearing this really nice new suit, and riding on a ticket courtesy of Monica. He also had $400 in crisp bills in his pocket due to her generosity. She had faith in him, and there had been no possible way for him to save money at the seminary, which had long ago taken all his service severance pay when he had entered.

Monica, tall and slender, moving with the grace of a fashion model in her dark beauty, had entranced him soon after he had arrived at the Temple Schools late in 1953, immediately after mustering out. He had met her while working at the reception desk at the YMCA, where he had gone to work to support himself at the Temple College. Her sister, Janine, was a bookkeeper at the Y, and he had met her first. Then, when Monica had come to visit her sister, he and Monica had struck up a beautiful friendship. Through her faith in him and his ability, she had encouraged him—and more, financed him, with what small help his parents could give him—to take this fateful trip to Hollywood.

Now he leaned back in the bus seat as comfortably as possible and let his mind wander back to those days in the beginning of his studies at Temple. He remembered his arrival. It had been deep in the night when the bus had whisked him, a newly discharged veteran, into Chattanooga. He had felt the city was something out of *Gone with the Wind.* He had smelled the magnolia blossoms that filled the air, felt the heat of the night, and observed the leisurely activity of the people—something he had never dreamed of in Michigan. He found it heady, and to a twenty-two-year-old Korean veteran, it was overpoweringly romantic.

While he would not say that his love for Monica was love at first sight, he had been attracted to her. But the very idea of love frightened him. He had an aversion to intimacy, and it was extremely hard for him to be really close to anyone. He was fully aware that as soon as he began to feel attraction to any girl, he ran. He didn't even question that now. It was simply a fact.

He had run from Monica—from intimacy with her. But she had drawn him near her with her graciousness, her beautifully drawn features and high cheekbones, and her queenly grace and charm that conquered his shyness. She had asked for so little.

They had met through Janine, her sister, and had seemed to relate to each other in a good-humored, spirited way. This had reassured him. And he was also aware that they both had scrupulously obeyed the official policy at the Temple Schools of "no skin on skin before marriage." He smiled now, remembering his later discovery that they had been the only ones at the school naive enough to take the rule seriously and the only ones who had obeyed the letter of the law.

He wondered about this for a moment now, but the thoughts of other girls flitted through his mind. And even while he was crediting Monica with being a beautiful, selfless soul who had encouraged him immensely—not only spiritually, but also materially—and really believed in him, his face flushed a little. His mind admitted that he had not always been as true to her in his emotions as he might have been. She was a good cook and had often brought him food when he was working as night clerk at the local YMCA. But he was haunted by whether she was God's choice, because she seemed so right, and could not decide as yet that she was his own final choice.

There had been other girls. He had become something of a Christian playboy at the school, maintaining, he assured himself, a good reputation but enjoying the company of quite a variety of girls. Still, he was here on this bus because of Monica, and he had to admit that. All the other girls were gone now. Monica was the one who was still with him.

There had been June. He squirmed now and changed his position. June had been the one who had really knocked him off his feet, he reminisced, thinking of her and conceding that she was a perfectly gorgeous girl. He admitted that she was everything he had ever dreamed of and more. She entered a room like Loretta Young coming on the screen, and his heart leaped now as he thought of her. Her beauty lit up a whole room. She was a gleaming jewel. She was a flickering candle flame to a moth.

He recalled how he had tried to manage an introduction when he had seen her sitting near him in the school library. After attempting to keep his nose in his books, he had found it too much. He knew she was a music teacher, so he decided to make an original overture. On a piece of copy paper, he drew a music staff and composed a few bars of music; then, as he strolled by, he had dropped it beside her on the table. Managing to get back to his seat without falling down, he awaited her reaction.

She rewarded him with a generous smile, but that was all. He hadn't the nerve to follow up this lead and introduce himself. Instead, he had gathered up his books and fled. Later, he had had the opportunity to meet her formally. He found she was even more attractive on closer acquaintance. Here was a glamorous girl who really gave him a strange and pleasurable sensation to be near. But she was engaged, he had heard. She hadn't told him so, and she invited his admiration and showed him in many thrilling little ways that she was also very attracted to him.

Sometimes, after a while, they seemingly accidentally met in the book stacks, where in the quiet privacy provided there, he would hold her close and kiss her marvelously soft lips. She molded herself to him so sweetly that he was overcome with emotion and a sensation he could not deny. He could have held her and kissed her forever, but someone inevitably wandered into their aisle, and the kisses would have to end.

But he did become almost painfully aware that normal human biology had not passed him by and that he very much enjoyed a closer intimacy than he had ever known. He had not realized it could be so pleasurable. And to his own surprise, he was gripped by an emotion that had hitherto been totally under his own control. But now he found that while much in life can be controlled by effort of will, this emotion was not as easily suppressed as others, and he was as tempted as any man under its spell. Infatuation had possessed him, body and soul, at this time. He knew he was violating the strict rule of the Temple, but strangely, he felt no sense of sin. Being close wasn't nearly as scary as he had thought. It was fun. It made him happy and seemed so right.

But as things had gone along, he met a different kind of girl. Charlotte's beauty had been of the spirit. She was anything but a glamour girl; she was a serious girl who worked in the snack bar on the campus. He had met her when he first came to the school, and they had become friends—mostly through Gary's efforts. He had been able to find a thousand different reasons to slip into the snack bar when Charlotte Ellis was there. She was his first real sweetheart, so called by other students and by himself.

She was a plain and ordinary-looking girl, but she had a charm that had swept him off his feet at once. He realized he cared for her, and this rather scared him, as he was far from experienced with girls. He could only show deep respect for her, as his parents had taught him. He made no advances to her, but he loved her from afar, so to speak.

He did not feel tied to her in any way and considered himself free to date other girls if he chose. He did not hesitate to "fall in love" with the beauteous and glamorous June or to be seen with other girls on the campus as he chose. Somehow, he had believed that when he grew tired of being the campus playboy, as he had been called (and he fancied the title), he would go back to Charlotte, and she, being "good" and not flirtatious in any way, would be waiting for him.

It did not occur to him and came as a complete and shocking surprise that she had found out about the clandestine meetings he was having with the more forward and beautiful June, even though she was an engaged girl. Someone had tattled, and Charlotte was deeply hurt, because it had been made plain to the entire student body of the campus that she and Gary were going steady with every intention of both supposedly aiming at a future marriage. But future to Gary was taken literally, and this was the present, and he had been ensnared by the obvious charm of June and had become infatuated with her.

He knew his association with June was limited, but Charlotte did not, and perhaps she did not care, in the face of her hurt. She had a sweet spirit and was loving and considerate. But he lost her completely in the explosion that occurred when she had found out about his clandestine meetings with June. He had tried to smooth things over, but she would not tolerate this, and the next time they met, she had announced her forthcoming marriage to another.

He had been crushed and heartsick. He could not believe that Charlotte, whom he felt he had really come to love, would leave him for so paltry a reason. Surely she knew that June would soon be married to someone else, and what could a few thrilling kisses mean compared to how he felt about someone like her, whom he truly loved? It was still a mystery to him, as he sat swaying in the bus seat on his way to Hollywood, why she had become so upset, so incensed, over nothing. Hadn't she known he loved her?

But she had turned upon him, crying bitterly, "After the way I've seen you walking around the campus with other girls and acting as if I didn't even exist, I would kill myself before I would consider going out with you again!" This was a crushing blow to Gary, who was not the Don Juan he appeared to be. It had hurt him deeply and left him devastated and mournfully regretful.

He tried to make her understand about his fickle affair with June. He tried to keep her from misunderstanding him and his intention. He had pleaded with her. But she had misunderstood, and though he had begged her to forgive him and to not marry on the rebound, as he felt she surely must be doing, she was adamant and had gone right on through with it. She married the nonentity of a man whom he could not imagine her married to. (Others could not believe it, either.) Well, she would regret it, he told himself, stirring in remembered misery, as he recalled that he had sat up one whole night and cried about her.

But he had recovered, and not long after, he had felt his dramatic urge pushing him to produce an act of Dickens's *A Christmas Carol* on the large stage in the gymnasium at the Temple School. He received permission to do so from Dr. Lee Roberson, president of Temple Schools and pastor of the Highland Park Baptist Church, and he became completely absorbed in it.

It had proven to be such a success that it was repeated the following year, and his head had been in the clouds. He had never expected to be on a bus on his way to Hollywood to play the part of Christ in a major motion picture. But here he was, and the bus was carrying him closer and closer to that magic city where make-believe was real. This road could lead him only toward the stairway to the stars, which he would soon climb, and he would shine among them.

Chapter 5

College Drama

Am I crowding the elderly gentleman beside me? Gary wondered. He remembered back to the very beginning of this incredible adventure he was speeding toward. He had been attending to his chapel duties, which were considerable, all during the time he had been staying at the Temple Schools. And through his presentation of the Christmas play of Dickens's *A Christmas Carol,* he had become known as something of a theatrical personality at school. He had still kept up his duties and responsibilities, meanwhile, in the small pastorate of the Stanley Baptist Chapel, conducting two services each Sunday, plus a midweek prayer meeting, and holding them in a unique place.

The wooden building was a small, one-room schoolhouse during the week. It contained two short rows of desks and a few folding chairs. A coal stove, which had no doubt seen the original settling of the country, still supplied the heat. But in contrast to this, some enterprising people had installed a flank of modern florescent light fixtures on the low ceiling barely overhead, which gave the place a dazzling, glaring atmosphere, altogether startling in that rustic setting.

The pulpit, necessarily removable, was of stark, utilitarian quality, but Gary had not minded any of this. He had seen God worshipped in Jeeps, in foxholes, and in war-torn open areas, and he felt that this chapel was more than adequate.

The natural beauty of the country had compensated for much and was a constant reminder to him of the gifts of our Creator. Waldon's Ridge in the Suck Creek community was a glorious backdrop, with wooded hills in the distance, complete with the Tennessee River lazily meandering by.

It was a small community, with a membership of some thirty-eight mountain people constituting his ministry. They attended services in cotton print dresses and overalls, and their simplicity was touching. They would not have believed that people in other parts of the country got dressed up to go to church. Mother's breastfed their babies during the sermons, and the fathers kept one iron hand free and ready to quiet any noisy children with them in the pews.

God was as real and as natural to these people as the woods and the hills that surrounded them. Talk about Him had to be straight and to the point. They were not interested in theology, philosophy, psychology, or eschatology. They liked God, and they liked Him talked about simply. They were not interested in a lot of talk about life and death. They'd seen enough of the first and took God at His word about the latter. When a baby was born in the mountains, they saw it happen. And when a relative died, they prepared him, made the coffin themselves, and put it in the ground personally.

They needed no lessons about how God worked in nature. They knew God's love in its natural form and returned it in like form with good measure. Gary remembered those simple services and how honored he had felt to serve in this small, pristine chapel.

He had also heard stories about the mountain people making moonshine back in the hills and how they settled disputes over it with shotguns. He was aware of what good marksmen they were and had felt he knew quite enough to satisfy himself by leaving that subject alone.

He remembered that one of his first responsibilities had been to visit a family who had lost a loved one that winter. It got very cold in the mountains, and the snow was deep. The mortuary was chilly, and everyone wore coats. He had gone to offer solace, and when he was leaving, he noticed the body of an elderly woman laid out in another room. It had made him sad that no one was viewing this body, so he went in and signed the guest book.

He approached the casket. As he drew near, he felt somewhat ill at ease, because he did not know the lady. An unearthly hissing sound rose out of the casket, and wraithlike clouds of vapor rose slowly from it. That was probably the shortest visitation in history. Gary found himself outside the room, out of the mortuary, and in his car before he came to himself. He smiled, watching those swift antics in retrospect in his mind's eye, still feeling a twinge of the mortal terror that had possessed him at that time.

It had only been later, on his way home, driving in a sort of daze, that he had suddenly realized there must have been a steam radiator against the wall behind the coffin that had happened to let off steam at that terribly inadvertent moment. And more untimely it could not have been, he concluded, feeling again the icy chill that had run up his back.

He became aware that the man seated next to him on the bus was glancing at him and realized he must look somewhat strange, smiling and almost chuckling to himself. But he did not feel he wanted to share this distant experience with a stranger, so he said a pleasant word or two, hoping the distinguished-looking elderly gentleman would think him not too eccentric. But the man evidently felt that a young man was entitled to his own private joke and did not appear to be in the least curious. Gary settled back, realizing he had little rapport with his silent seatmate, and went back to his reverie about the area of his life.

He remembered his newness to his ministry as well as his newness to those mountain people whom he was attempting to instruct without the slightest need, since he felt they were even more devout than he. All in all, he thought, if they learned anything from him, it was a credit only to God. He certainly had not known what he was doing. He slid down further in his seat, swallowing his chagrin, and then remembered why he was here, whirling past the countryside instead of attending those erstwhile ministerial duties of his.

It had been in his senior college year that his attention had been drawn by others to an item mentioned by the popular Hollywood columnist Louella Parson, who told in one of her articles about the largest film company in Hollywood planning to present a great production based on the religious theme of the life of Jesus Christ. It was to be called *The Greatest Story Ever Told.* The very name of the production had thrilled him.

He was the one they were looking for. He was about to become a minister, and his dream had always been to be an actor. What better role to burst forth into his full glory than himself in the role of his beloved Jesus?

It had been like a dream come true. Gary had gone about in a daze after that. He felt chosen. He felt there was not the slightest possibility of anyone else being more suited to the role than he. True, he was not an experienced movie actor, but they wanted an unknown, didn't they? And he was the right size and the right age—twenty-four. He had fairly dark hair and could grow a beard, and if Jesus was to be pictured as having dark, wavy hair, a wig could do that. If Jesus' eyes were brown to match his hair and his Jewish blood, so that? He had seen many a blue-eyed picture and statue of Jesus. And he had seen many with light brown hair, and while his hair was straight, it could be waved or even curled, and it could grow if they wanted it long. And there was always a wig. There was no excuse. He was Jesus. Somehow, he had to get that part. He felt it was his destiny.

Acting was a learned ability. He could learn, he told himself, and he had always had a good memory. Living in Hollywood would be expensive. But he had to go. God would show him the way. And he prayed to Jesus fervently, believing in Christ's miracles.

This was God's plan for him, he felt. He felt it in his very soul. What a wonderful thing Jesus was doing for him, making it possible for him to satisfy his two great passions—being a minister and being an actor. He had always wanted both. Now the way was opening up. This message was for him. They were looking expressly for him. But how in the world could he get their attention?

He would have to forget it, he had told himself at first, and now he writhed a little in his seat as he remembered the agony of not being able to forget it. He felt he was not supposed to forget it. And he had begun to feel a most compelling urge to act upon this opportunity—this pointed invitation.

It was meant for him and him only. No one else in the world was a more natural choice. He felt he was being chosen by God to strive to do this thing—almost that it was created solely for his efforts. It was perfect for him—his rightful destiny. But he was helpless. Now he became the Prodigal Son, begging, "Give me the portion of good that falleth to me."

He wanted so badly to go to that far country of Hollywood in California that he thought of nothing else. But he had not thought about the part where the Bible says, "There arose a mighty famine in that land." And he had forgotten that the wayward son "would fain have filled his belly with the husks that the swine did eat."

All this was beside the point. The point was that this was the opportunity of his lifetime at a time when he was strapped to his duties, to the most monotonous of lives—that of a country minister, borne down by the set of his ideas of his congregation far more rigorously than any slave to his master. There was no room in his life as a minister to this rigid flock for any deviation, and there was no tolerance for any innovative changes from the straight and narrow for their beloved minister. He was their idol and their tool. He was as devoid to them of human qualities as any graven image and as rigidly ruled by their limited desires as any idol molded of clay.

They were not aware of this, Gary admitted to himself. He had placed himself within their path, had studied under the most avid of Protestant ministers in the school of his choice, so what complaint had he that was valid? Valid or not, the feeling he had had was one of desperate longing for release, and no one could dream of more release than being swallowed up in the secular society of the greatest dreamland in the world—Hollywood.

Everyone wanted to go to Hollywood and become a movie star. It was a dream of almost every living soul on earth who had ever heard of this fantastic wonderland. Hollywood was a place where love was so graciously and generously expressed that the entire world loved Hollywood. All the goods of an affluent world were thrown at the feet of those who were successful. Who would not want to taste these glamorous and alluring sweets?

He had dreamed of this, but he had also dreamed of carrying out a mission for the Lord. He was going to this wonderland not only to taste the honey, but also to spread the Word—the wonderful Word of God. Surely, no one else who dreamed of playing the part of Christ in the forthcoming wonderful production would enable the entire world to see and know what Christ was really like with anywhere near such truth as he would strive to do.

He stretched out his tired legs, and seeing that his seatmate on the bus was sleeping quietly, went back to the events that had led him to this seat beside a dozing gentleman who might soon be recognizing him on a wide screen in a darkened movie theater. This thought gave him new courage, and his thoughts went back to the miracle that God had arranged in order to bring him here to this confining seat on this swiftly moving bus.

At first, it had all seemed so helpless. He was an unknown and doomed to be an unknown to the end of time. He was aware that he should accept this and pay attention only to his ministerial duties. He had at least made up his mind to do this. But others were working the mysteries of Gods wisdom for him when he himself could not. He had been surprised to discover, very soon after Louella's column had announced the search for an unknown, that others were also thinking of his fitness for the part.

He had sent a clipping of the column to his parents and his sister, Janice, who remembered his early success as actor, singer, announcer, and disc jockey. They all felt he was especially chosen for the part. They believed he would play it with the sincerity it deserved. They strongly encouraged him to act upon this sign of God's approval and to make every effort to make himself known to the producers of this coming production. He would be the ideal answer to their problem and would make his relatives very proud to have a movie actor in the family.

Of course, he could understand this, but all they were able to offer in the way of performing the miracle it would take was encouragement. It had helped, but it could not do the trick. He would have to attract the producer's attention. And to do that, he must present himself personally in Hollywood. In the meantime, however, things had been working out on the side. He had become so desperate to make his presence known from afar that he had taken the bull by the horns, so to speak, and had become his own press agent.

He smiled now as he remembered his trepidation in writing to the great Walter Lang, the Twentieth Century-Fox director who would direct *The Greatest Story Ever Told.* He had described himself, his background, and his fervent ambition to the considered for the role.

Walter Lang had answered his letter. He had answered it kindly, and they had begun a correspondence about the subject. Suddenly, the story of this correspondence was ferreted out and reported in an Associated Press release on March 19, 1957 in the *Chattanooga Times.*

This told the world. The item had explained that though there had been no casting as yet and it would be at least a year before production would start, Gary Heikkila, an undergraduate student at Temple Schools, was being seriously considered for the lead part of Jesus in the forthcoming production.

Stanley Chapel and Temple Schools immediately became popular with the local news media, which pointed out in various articles on the subject that it was not often a Temple Schools graduate went off to Hollywood to star in a picture. In fact, it had never happened before. And Gary still felt the pleasure of being singled out as a prominent and newsworthy figure. He sat up a little straighter in this bus seat now as the gentleman beside him slumbered on.

Reporters had soon begun visiting the chapel services and calling the school for more information about him, he remembered, and the *Chattanooga Free Press* really had gone all out. A reporter had written an enthusiastic full report on him, which he had cut out, folded carefully, and now carried in his wallet. He took it out now, and in the boredom of the bus carrying its passengers through the flat prairie lands of the southern Midwest, he unfolded the clipping and read it. It began,

> Inside the small wooden chapel which serves as a schoolhouse during the week, a young minister was recounting to his congregation the age-old story of Christ's Passion. The voice of Russell Gary Heikkila carried powerfully and commandingly across the one room of Stanley Baptist Chapel, and his outward poise concealed the mental strain which the Tennessee Temple Senior had been subjected to in recent weeks. Heikkila, with the possibility to play the role of Christ in the Twentieth Century-Fox forthcoming production of *The Greatest Story Ever Told,* had been unsure until recently over whether to accept the opportunity to play the part, should it be offered …
>
> Heikkila told this writer that after much prayer and consultation with various individuals, his mind is now definitely made up. He said he would welcome the opportunity to show the world through a film that Jesus Christ is a living, ever-present reality and was able to do for us what we are unable to do for ourselves—bring salvation, joy, and peace that passeth all understanding.
>
> Heikkila, however, emphasized that he had no plans of pursuing a stage career should this opportunity be realized but hopes to one day establish an orphanage in Korea, where he won the Bronze Star for service during the Korean conflict … The movie for which Heikkila is being considered is to be based on the book by Fulton Ousler.
>
> Heikkila, who pays his way through school by working part-time at the Central YMCA, would very much like to win the top role of the movie for which Holly wood

is seeking an amateur, but his ultimate aim is toward a smaller but more important stage, say about pulpit-size.

Then, as the bus began to slow and turn off the highway for the evening dinner stop, he folded the news item and replaced it in his wallet.

Dinner was a hurried affair, and soon they were all back on the bus. Then, after a short conversation about mundane subjects, the gentleman in the seat beside him bowed his head and lost himself again in sleep. Gary's mind slipped back to the time when the news items in all the papers had informed everyone in the school and Stanley Chapel of his intent to take the part of Jesus and remove himself to that iniquitous city on the rim of the Pacific Ocean, which was predicted to be on the verge of falling into the sea in the very near future. It was agreed upon that this was to be God's retribution for the sins committed there by the unholy who resided in and around that wicked place called Hollywood.

Gary had begun to receive letters from anti-Hollywood people after that item had appeared, asking him, "If God called you to be a minister, why are you stooping so low as to be an actor?" Gary was aware that actors never had merit in the eyes of mountain people, and religion was so much a part of their lives that anything as remote from their religious beliefs as the actors in Hollywood, whom they viewed as part of the Devil's pawn, was not to be thought of. And certainly their own dear minister would most surely not seriously think of joining this dissolute world.

But he did not plan to join the Hollywood scene—only to put himself into this one part, where he would have the best chance of his lifetime to show the whole world what Jesus was really like. He felt he knew. And given the chance, he would convey to the world the wonders of Jesus. He would be Jesus' worldly emissary. This was a supreme chance to show what Jesus was really like—to make Jesus human to the world of today. It was a mission.

He felt that most people saw Jesus as a distant figure in biblical history, while Gary, through his studies and prayers, had come to see Jesus as a real human being—a friend of man to mankind. It would be a truly glorious opportunity for him to convey his own feelings of oneness with Christ to the audience that flocked to the movies.

People loved movies. They liked nothing more. What better chance would anyone ever have to bring Jesus to them as a living, breathing human being, as Jesus really was? His own love for Jesus would come shining through in this part, he felt, and the divine love that Jesus has for mankind would surely shine out from the face of one who loved Jesus as he did. He could not let anyone else play this part, because it was his calling to play it. It was his personal offering to Jesus. It would be his token of love. His love and understanding of the humanness of the Lord Jesus would pour out to the world, and they could not help responding.

And so, he assured himself, it was not for the glory or riches of Hollywood that he wanted to play this part. It was to proclaim to the Lord his love and devotion and to receive His loving grace. He had felt certain from the first that God was guiding him, and he still felt certain as he shifted his position in the bus seat. He searched his mind for any other motive and found none.

He was not afraid of what the negative letters had warned him—that Hollywood would sweep him away in a total wave of transgressions of which he was not even aware yet in his limited experience. Surely our Lord, who had walked constantly with the publicans and sinners, would strengthen him in the face of Hollywood's temptations.

His mind went back now to when he had finished his senior year and had been ordained. It had been on May 25, 1956, and the ceremony had made a deep impression upon him. "Russell Gary Heikkila, solemnly and publicly set apart and ordained to do the work of the gospel ministry …" It had been wonderfully fulfilling at that time to know he had dedicated his life to the work of the Lord.

The fifteen men on the ordaining council had come and laid hands upon those being ordained and prayed for God's blessing and benediction upon them. Had it been only a coincidence that Dr. Lee Roberson had chosen 2 Corinthians 12:7–10 as the text for the ordination sermon? "There was given me a thorn in my flesh, a messenger of Satan to torment me."

Was he now being carried to that buffeting—that thorn? Gary wondered this as he looked over the bus full of people and knew that of them all, he was the only one who was an ordained minister and the only one who was on his way to Hollywood with the hope—the assurance—of playing a star role in a marvelous picture about the life of Christ.

He felt ready to explode, but he sat quietly and remembered how the conflict over his going to Hollywood had intensified as his departure time had approached. His close friends had encouraged him in every way, but it had been Monica whom God had used to supply the money, undreamed of and unattainable by himself for the trip.

Dear Monica believed in him as he believed in himself and supplied not only the ticket, but also a new suit and $400 in crisp, new bills straight from the bank. Monica not only believed in him, but also was willing to back him. *Wonderful Monica,* he thought as he remembered her face with the saintly look of faith and sacrifice upon it and love shining out from her eyes. He hoped this constant riding was not going to wrinkle the suit to a degree that dry cleaning would not be able to restore.

He had written ahead to the YMCA in Los Angeles to reserve a room and also had written to the major studios that he was arriving. Of course, he realized, it was not exactly like announcing the appearance of Richard Burton, but he had made them aware of his correspondence with Walter Lang and of his invitation to a screening, and he had received kind replies and invitations, so he felt fairly well prepared.

But after spending the second night on the bus, passing through the upper part of Texas, and long before he reached Los Angeles, he was worn and tired, and he wondered if this was not the Lord's way of teaching him patience, longsuffering, and forbearance, since he was grinning very little and only just bearing it. There was no rest. On and on, mile after mile, for nearly three thousand miles, he was tossed and bruised, off and on busses at the most inconvenient times—in the middle of the night, cold early mornings, with one torturing three-hour layover between buses. The stop was not long enough to get a hotel room and too long to stay awake. So he huddled and dozed on a hard bus station bench. Along the way, he drank tepid water from rusty fountains, ate stale donuts, and drank vile coffee at early morning openings of bus depot cafes. He wondered what he was doing there.

But once back on the bus, he always felt better, and he passed the time by playing his new role of movie star to the passengers, signing small note pads for little old ladies who wanted his autograph and who promised to watch faithfully day and night till they saw his handsome face before them as the Lord on their twelve-inch black-and-white screens at home. That part was rather fun, he thought, and he made comments to a new seatmate, a young salesman going home from a long route of selling razor blades to sundry stores. He was untalkative, Gary thought, for a salesman, and he guessed the salesman wasn't doing too well by comparing suits.

After five long, torturous days, it ended. The bus depot was in Los Angeles and nowhere near Hollywood. It seemed instead a Mecca for winos and bums. Located in a very rundown part of the city, it offered a painful surprise in the numbers of panhandlers who mistook his new suit for the garb of a rich and generous man.

Since he was neither, he shooed them off as best he could and set out on foot for the YMCA. As he walked along, he decided that Los Angeles did not, at least in that area, inspire visions of stardom. It presented rather a somber scene of busy, silent people hustling past each other, eyes forward, glancing at no one. So Gary, quite aware of his vulnerability, did not disturb or try to delay these zombie-like creatures but walked steadily on, carrying two heavy suitcases in the hot June sun until he came to the large, imposing edifice of the YMCA.

He had realized at the depot that there would be no parade in honor of his arrival, but he was not prepared for the shock of the prices of rooms at the YMCA. He had thought that people stayed at such places and away from plush hotels to save money. But one would save very little at this YMCA. At these rates, he would be lucky to have enough money to last him two weeks.

His room was almost a suite, however, and beautifully appointed. He would have liked to stay there and bask in this atmosphere. It gave him the strength to believe in anything. But the price was truly frightening.

Chapter 6

Twentieth Century-Fox

As soon as he was settled in his room, he rested for that day, going out only to eat a good, expensive meal. The next morning, however, he went out early to locate a bus that would take him to Hollywood. The bus took over a half hour to arrive in Hollywood, and he went first to Twentieth Century-Fox, a bit starry-eyed. He had been led to expect, after all that writing back and forth, that he would be welcome.

But there was no one there who knew who he was, and no one who cared. Walter Lang was not available. Everyone else was busy, concentrating on what had to be done in a hurry. Not one person paid any attention to him. No one was at ease, and no one slowed down for a moment. They rushed on to the end of the day and disappeared into thin air, leaving an empty world of silence behind them. Rushing, panting, running, shouting, going into seizures of emotion and apoplectic anger and then coming out smoothly, they seemed to be in a world of their own. Gary was an outsider, and no one knew who he was or cared in any way at all. He went back the next day and was again shunted aside and ignored.

On about the third day of pushing, shoving, and being promised help "in a minute," which dragged into hours, he was told what everyone else seemed to know. *The Greatest Story* was bogged down in endless scripting problems, he finally gathered. The general consensus, he found out still later, was that it would be more than a year before it was ready for production, and it might never be ready. All this was a great shock and very discouraging for a young man from a considerate, respectful, orderly, slow-paced seminary world with only a little money and no way to make more in this mad, strange, hectic place.

He fell into a conversation at last with a man who introduced himself as the publicist for the studio. The man was surprisingly friendly and considerate. Fran Neil proved to be a real friend indeed. He took Gary to dinner at the studio commissary and arranged for him to be photographed with the very popular star of the FBI pictures as well as of other leading parts, Robert Stack.

This, Gary knew, would give him the kind of publicity he needed, and he was more determined than ever to crash the gates of dreamland and become a full-fledged Hollywood actor while he waited for his part in *The Greatest Story.* No matter how long he had to wait for the part, he would find a way, he told himself. He would wait and never give up.

The glamour of Hollywood had hooked him as soon as he had entered an actual set. This one was the set for *The Gift of Love* with Lauren Bacall and Robert Stack. Lauren Bacall, who was even more beautiful than in her picture, was upset about a scene. She was distant and left the set as soon as her scene was over, but Robert Stack was friendly and easily persuaded to pose with him. That was the thrill of a lifetime for Gary. He wanted now more than ever to make a name for himself in the movies. He had been there a scant three days, but he had learned much.

First, he had to find a cheaper place to live. At the end of the week, he had found a small apartment near the Y. The efficiency apartment room was small, containing only the barest minimum of furniture and less comfort, but he promised himself he would not be there long, and it was cheap.

He saw doors opening all around him in Hollywood, and so with confidence, he engaged an agent. Why not? How would one hope to become successful without one? He was asked on every side. Everyone had an agent. That was the secret. The Theater Arts Agency on Sunset Boulevard was recommended. It was small enough, he was told, to give him personal attention. That was a big advantage; the agency convinced him when he went to inquire. And they had him signed up before he had made up his mind. But that was best, he thought; since he would have been much more hesitant had he been given time to think of the cost. It was done now, and his work of being exposed was begun at once.

His very first instructions were to keep his religious background in the background. It would do him no good at all to let anyone know he was a minister. Ministers were not popular with people in Hollywood. Part of this was because the majority were Jewish—certainly all of the big shots were Jewish, and these included all the producers, directors, and so forth—so a Baptist minister was not likely to be one of their favorite people, he was informed. And those who were not Jewish were atheists or agnostics. No one had time for God in spite of all the fervent praying they did for parts.

Gary told himself he should have expected this. Had he not been warned? He would either have to accept these circumstances or run back to his ministry and give up the idea of Hollywood entirely. He felt he could learn to conform to what was evidently the way things were. But he would certainly have a harder time in converting these people than he had expected. Still, this must not deter him.

He had come to play the part of Jesus in a way that would bring Jesus to the people who saw the picture. He would not even have the opportunity to play Christ if he ran away now. It might be a year or more before the picture went into production, he had heard, and if he stayed here, he would have a much better chance of getting the part than if he went home to wait the time out. No, he decided, he should stay and learn as much as he could about Hollywood and the profession of acting. Then he could be ready when the time came to walk into the part he was waiting for.

He need not be a part of Hollywood to stay and learn all he could. He could still keep his own values. From what he saw of the life there, one needed all one had. Most of the people there seemed to have little (if any) values whatsoever, he observed. He would be different in that respect. It was up to the individual, he reassured himself.

For several weeks, Gary kept his head and resisted the urgings of the agency to change his name to the more glamorous Garrison Gray. He thought the name was attractive but had planned to act under his own name. The agency, however, decided he needed another name, and they made him feel they expected great things of him.

How much better it would be, the publicity agent had suggested, if he were already a star—or at least a well-known actor—by the time *The Greatest Story* was ready for production? Then he would surely get the part, and he could then return to his real name and announce who he was—and so much the better. But in the meantime, if he wanted to be a star, he must conform to the rules, play the game, and let them handle him in their own way. It was imperative, he was told. And his own name lacked the necessary glamour.

Alone in his room, Gary thrilled at the idea of being a star. There were many parts around that he could fit if he knew the ropes and could become known as a steadily working actor. He had come to know by now that there was much to learn in this trade and that those who knew were the ones who were chosen for parts.

He changed his name now to the more euphonious and glamorous Garrison Gray, and with it, his personality had seemed to change spontaneously to match the character the name implied. He was amazed at the ease of this transformation but did not feel that it touched his innate nature. It was only a pseudonym that he had need of for the present.

He slowly began to adapt, long for parts, and feel the pull of the glamour that surrounded him. Then came the hectic pace of being seen by the big people at the "in" places. This was very important, he gathered, and he stilled his conscience by realizing the expediency of this. Each morning, he rode the bus to Hollywood. His agent took him to these "in" places and introduced him as the coming star of *The Greatest*

Story, for all it was worth. Friends he made along the way took him to other places, and his life soon became a constant parade of places.

For months, he went clubbing every night. It was exhilarating, and he carefully kept his religious vocation a deep secret, planning to admit it only when he was at last playing the part of Jesus in *The Greatest Story*, as the proposed picture was commonly called. He planned then to burst open in the world as his true self—a devout and everlasting believer and therefore the perfect actor to play the important part of Jesus in that proposed great picture. And as the star, his name would be forever remembered.

After that, of course, he would not need to worry about parts. They would come showering down upon him. His only problem then would be to exercise the proper discrimination in keeping his name free from any tarnish that would impede his spreading the word of God among these iniquitous people when the time came. And he was quickly certain that God had put him there for this specific purpose. He felt badly needed. But he felt the time was not right to do anything but to learn the ropes of Hollywood, and in so doing, give himself a rapport with the people he would lead to salvation when it was time.

He knew he must prepare himself if he was to exert any influence in this wayward and busy place—busy not only with the hectic pursuit of hedonistic happiness, but also with the pressing and vital business of obtaining money. He must join them or be forever outside the lexicon of their purposes and philosophy. This would place him far from any position of influence he would need to impress them later. But in the meantime, he was losing some of the strict sense of honor that had guided his life and to which he expected to return when his purpose for God in Hollywood was accomplished. That purpose, he felt more and more, was to lead these people from their sinful lives to the glory of true believers, who would cast all sin aside and lead faithful and sinless lives when he had converted them to the wonders of being saved. But now he dared not mention it.

Also, in the meantime, he asked himself as he dressed carefully to go out to nightclubs night after night, how would he know what he was saving them from if he did not now go out and learn the sins from which he would deliver them? This was all a part of his mission, he assured himself.

The sins he was being introduced to now had been totally unknown to him. He knew sins vaguely, but he was in a position now, for once in his life (and indeed for the first and perhaps only time in his life he would ever have, he assured himself) to learn of the actual sins these people committed. In spite of his Army service, he was naive. He was, he had to admit, downright ignorant. These sins were quite different from those he had heretofore encountered.

His naiveté showed so plainly that one studio official took it upon himself to inform Gary of the bitter truth. The official assured him of the shocking fact that when they looked for the perfect type to cast for a pure virgin maiden; they looked for a prostitute to play the part. They were the most convincing to the audience, he said. And when they wanted someone to play a call-girl, they picked the most virgin and moral actress they could find. They looked more like real call-girls. And when they wanted someone to play a preacher, a minister or the role of a priest, they picked the most dissolute of actors, and for villains, the most moralistic and reputable of men.

Perhaps, the agent suggested to Gary, that he, being a large man, could get anti-hero, bad man parts while he waited for his big part. "Or, since you're tall and handsome, you might play the lothario type. You might even become a new Tyrone Power, or even Rudy Valentino, the greatest of them all," he coaxed. While Gary was aghast, his agent continued blithely, "Yes, that's what you should try for. You could very easily become a sexy leading man; you have those romantic bedroom eyes!" Gary had never even heard the expression before, but he gathered what it meant and felt a deep revulsion.

Still, some of the words were beautiful to Gary. He knew he was tall and reasonably good-looking, but he had never imagined anyone would take him seriously as a romantic leading man—until he had come to Hollywood, and here, a director was telling him just that. It must be true. And he would certainly not turn down such a part.

But no actual part developed at that time. He waited and took care to get all the exposure he could. And he missed no opportunities for a screening. He came so close to a part at times that he knew it was only a matter of patience. And he was developing a great deal of that.

Chapter 7

This Gun for Hire

Is it not the Christian's duty to infiltrate? Gary asked himself. Should not a true witness for the Lord walk down every avenue and explore even the depth of life? How could one save people of whom one knew nothing? How could sins be exonerated through a minister who did not know what the sins he was asking God to forgive were?

How could a minister ask the heavenly Father to forgive sins that were not even known by a minister? How effective could a pastor be in intervening for the sinner and begging for forgiveness for sins of which he knew nothing? So, did it not behoove a pastor to be aware—to know of sins? He asked himself this. And where better than Hollywood? But still, he buried his head in his pillow and wept, asking only for strength to bear his burden of want, poverty, and loss of dignity, not for forgiveness for any sins of theirs or of his own. Not yet. There was much further to go before that, and he had barely started.

He thought he felt the hand of God guiding him when he was called to a screening for the remake of *This Gun for Hire.* This picture had originally starred Veronica Lake and Alan Ladd. Now it was being done again with Bob Ivers, a newcomer in the Ladd role in this new version.

Bob was very cordial and pleasant after the screening, and Gary met the other stars in the film later at a studio party. They were all nice and very friendly and were so relaxed and natural it was hard for Gary to believe he was meeting these great personalities, whom he had just watched on the screen, face to face. All this was very satisfying, and he felt he was getting on the inside.

At another time, on the set of *The Matchmaker* with Shirley Booth and Anthony Perkins, he spoke with an extra who had been in Hollywood for some fifteen years. He told Gary, conveying admiration, that he himself had not rubbed elbows with half the stars Gary had become acquainted with in just a few months. He said Gary should consider himself as having quite an "in" by knowing all the well-established stars he knew. This made Gary feel as if he might really be getting somewhere in this baffling business that was so different from any other on earth. He was learning to play the game.

Now he began to feel nothing for himself or other people. The struggle to survive had grown so intense that it was all there was. He had one idea and one only—to succeed somehow, by any means. He felt that only by his success would he ever redeem himself from where he had already slipped. But he kept on slipping further into the depth of the voracious, consuming fire of his dream.

While Gary liked the women he met, at this point, he used them only as companions to make his appearances for the sake of his image. This image was fast becoming in his mind that of a torrid romantic hero of the Tyrone Power type—a passionate Don Juan whom no woman could resist. He had been told that he had boudoir eyes, and this personality fitted the name he had assumed, Garrison Gray.

For this Garrison Gray image, he was not only losing touch with any spiritual life, but also actually withdrawing from the world around him. Immersed in people, he was frantic with loneliness. While surrounded by love as he was, he felt the awful loneliness of not belonging to anyone, not being himself, and not even knowing who he was. His days were empty, and his nights were spent in a garish party atmosphere or alone in his room, miserable and not daring to think. He found he was only trying to pass the time somehow until the next screening, party, or nightclub date, where he might make a contact. This frenetic attending had become his life.

It was during this time that he met Marlon Brando's father at Paramount Studios. They talked for some time about the ministry after Gary had inadvertently confessed to him the real reason he was in Hollywood. Brando's father believed this and told Gary that Marlon had wanted to be a minister before he had become an actor. Afterward, Gary thought that over and found it a little anomalous that Marlon had wanted to be what he was, and he so desperately wanted to be what Marlon was. This was indeed a strange world, he concluded.

He had been very careful not to reveal the fact that he was a minister to anyone else, because he was very busy building up his image as Garrison Gray, romantic lead and libidinous lothario, while he waited for his big part. And if he told one person, he told them all. Hollywood was a small town in that way. But it was becoming increasingly hard to keep the romantic leading man image going when he had no parts to further it. He also found that some people in Hollywood were not really very nice.

When he landed a chance for exposure on a local TV show, *Let's Dance,* the lady emcee had insidiously insisted on asking him about his spiritual life in a way that revealed she knew more than he had known she did. He soon realized that she was intent on making him confess in public what would have absolutely ruined his image as a romantic leading man. He saw with a feeling of sick horror that she would have done this with no compunction whatever, knowing full well what immense harm she was doing. He was learning to fear as well as admire during his hectic sojourn in celluloid land.

He thought in hunted terror, of how this would have affected his future in Hollywood had he succumbed to her prying questions and given himself away He would have been finished, because at that time, he had a dream of becoming the reincarnation of the most romantic hero of them all, Rudolph Valentino.

Into his desperate mind had crept a way of breaking through in Hollywood. He had tried all the means he knew of, and he was doing all of the right things. He had hired an agent, and he had taken acting lessons from an excellent teacher, Helen Thayler, a well-known drama coach. He was being seen at all the right places. He had met many of the people who were the right people to meet, and he had exposed himself freely. His life was filled with really exciting moments he would not have missed for anything. And he had the feeling he would be discovered at any moment. So he must not relax, or all might be lost. The only thing wrong was that he was still not in the movies, and he did not seem to be getting there very fast.

He could not wait forever or even much longer. But he had happened upon a pure inspiration that came from somewhere, and he did not question it. He would abide by that inspiration. It might be divinely inspired, he felt, though he did not ask.

For months, ever since someone had remarked that his eyes reminded them of Valentino's eyes, he had been reading about the life of Valentino and of his wonderful success. Gradually, he had become imbued with the feeling that he might actually be—well, he had heard of reincarnation. Of course, his religion did not allow this concept, but his religion was far behind him now, and he was off on any hobbyhorse that would take him to stardom, regardless of how. More fantastic ideas than this had been furthered to success in Hollywood's fantasyland, he was aware. And here it was—the perfect vehicle. The world still loved Valentino and was still waiting for his return. Women were still longing for him.

He was mesmerized by his mission. That it was a far departure from the last mission for which he had felt a calling was not important. The world must give him a chance to be famous in order for him to have the authority of fame he needed to lead these people in their transversion from a sinful life to one of everlasting peace hereafter in being saved.

That his thinking was muddled did not occur to him. His purpose seemed clear, and he began to stand aside and let another part of his nature take control. He would keep a watchful eye on this newly inspired personality, he promised himself. He would be careful not to be led astray.

His thinking was that if he had to camouflage his original mission—if he had to commit transgressions, starve, and have no roof over his head—he must at least in the process perform his mission of achieving fame. Fame had become an obsession.

He made a pilgrimage to the grave of the great lover. He was gripped in such passionate desire to emulate and be the reincarnated lover that he was as in a dream, strolling mesmerized, gripped by a self-hypnotic fervor among the graves of bygone heroes resting in Forest Lawn Memorial Park, Hollywood. He walked among the beautiful mausoleums at the cemetery, seeing the final resting places of Tyrone Power, Douglas Fairbanks, Sr., and others, and Rudolph Valentino, king of lovers. Here he received such a spiritual uplift that he felt he had never been so happy before; yet a nagging voice in the back of his mind kept warning, *This happiness is not the truth.*

He stood mesmerized before Valentino's crypt. He saw the way now. He needed to inspire someone to help him portray this magnetic leading man on the screen, and he would sweep the audience away in a desire to see more and more of the masterful, passionate scenes they had so loved. He dreamed in the midst of the beauty of the mausoleum and carried his dreams away with him, home to his room. He slept with them, awoke with then, and let them consume him. But again, he heard that plans were being made to produce *The Greatest Story Ever Told.* He had not forgotten that. And he would never forget his primary mission, he told himself as he struggled out of confusion and back to some reality.

Chapter 8

The Greatest Story

Gary rushed to the studio to remind them again that he was still there, waiting to portray his first love—the role of Christ in this great forthcoming picture. They met him with discouraging news. *The Greatest Story* was still not making any progress. And all of his connections for playing the lead part were breaking up. He was told they were even thinking of selling the property to George Stevens, and if that happened, he planned to put the Swedish actor Max Von Sydow in the role of Christ. There was still a chance of it being produced by Twentieth Century-Fox, though not for some time, he learned.

In the meantime, he kept getting letters from Tennessee. Friends at the Temple Schools intruded upon the romantic image he now realized might be his only forte in Hollywood if the lead part of Christ in *The Greatest Story* was really gone. But it wasn't yet, and he clung to the hope that it would finally work out in some way for his good.

The letters he received from Tennessee did not make him feel better; they were depressing to him. He delayed opening them and sometimes hid them from his sight, especially while he was conscientiously dousing himself with cologne in preparation for a big evening out to further his career in the movie world. But when he found them later, he read them. And because he could not forget or ignore his friends, who had not forgotten him, he would weep for the lost security of the school he was so far from in the plastic world of tawdry glitter and capricious madness.

But he had to go on with his dream, because he might still get the part for which he had come to Hollywood. It was especially hard to go on, though, after a day of one frustrating disappointment after another, making the rounds of the studios, chasing false rumors of casting for parts in the glamorous world of make-believe, and going back for an evening of exposure and rapid gaiety without pleasure. In the morning, when he read the down-to-earth letters of Professor Hale, who wrote at times, he remembered another world.

Professor Hale of Temple Schools never gave up on Gary, never admonished him, and always showed good Christian fellowship. But Gary could read between the lines that the professor was praying constantly that he would finally get his fill of this false world that had beckoned him from his calling. He never really said so, but it was plain that his constant fear was that Gary would be spiritually swept away and become lost in the dens of iniquity he knew were waiting there for any stray spirit.

Perhaps Gary was lost for a time during the frantic nightclubbing phase when night after night, he went out in pursuit of the illusive "being discovered" through the exposure he sought. He often came home too late and too weary on Saturday night to attend church on Sunday morning. But from his first walk onto the Twentieth Century-Fox lot in the midst of wild confusion, he had been led through a maze of maddening delays. And having decided that he would not only wait for that part, but also would make a name for himself in movie land while he waited, he had plunged into the morass of make-believe that has drowned many. And now he was being consumed by an obsession that had only grown stronger with frustration and disappointment.

Paramount Studios had beckoned him shortly after his arrival by calling him to an audition there with the head of it, Frank Freeman, Jr. After only a few months in Hollywood, he had walked into the studio and been instantly overcome with the beauty of Freeman's secretary,

Golda. She was the most gorgeous girl he had ever seen. Why wasn't she a star? How could she not be? But she seemed quite happy with her job. She announced Gary's presence at once and escorted him in, walking so near him that he caught the scent of her perfume. A close look at her beautiful blonde hair, so perfectly and elaborately coiffured, made his knees weak. Gary decided then in those short moments that he, too, would one day have a gorgeous beauty like her in his own studio. They would notice him in Hollywood when he had established himself, as he intended to.

Freeman had seemed astonished when Gary had told him what had brought him to Hollywood. "You as Christ? Hell, no. You belong in bedrooms!" he had exploded. Gary had not been sure he meant it as a compliment, but he took it as one anyway.

If Freeman thought he could be a bedroom lothario, who was he to argue? Since his role of Christ was not yet ready, he had decided to do whatever he could in the meantime. So when Freeman gave him the script of an old Tyrone Power film, *The Razor's Edge,* and told him to memorize a scene for an audition at Paramount, he had been enchanted. But when he had rehearsed and memorized his scene to perfection, he found to his disappointment that he would not have a beautiful actress to play opposite him at the audition. He would have only an unattractive, middle-aged drama coach to read the lines back to him gruffly and unfeelingly.

It was a total letdown. She was a fine coach, he knew, but she was totally indifferent in her reading. She was also oblivious of the fact that this was his first launch into a great career. She simply threw the cues at him in a most casual way, which shook him, and the audition was a dismal failure. But shattered dreams were becoming routine to him by then, and he was hooked. His struggles were only to gratify his desires, not to escape.

The whole idea of Hollywood, he found, was to play the game. It was all a game, and there was no recess to the game. One played it night and day, day in and day out, year in and year out, and finally, to some, there was left no difference or distinction between reality and the game. Life became a total game, and one was finally absorbed in it, consumed by it, and lost to the world of reality. There were many lost people in Hollywood, he found. But he was determined not to be one of them.

The game was vicious. He would learn to play it, but he would remain aware that the game could not be all, for he would remember that there was another world that was very different. But he was not yet ready to give up the game, because he had not yet won. And it did not occur to him to wonder if he ever would. This was so absorbing a venture, and the stakes were so high, that the satisfaction of winning must be worthwhile, he concluded in his semi-lucid moments.

This was what he wanted—to be a winner. With concentration, effort, and grim determination, he could win, he knew. He felt it deep inside him. He did not mistake desire for the Holy Grail. He would lead the world to righteousness when he had created an authoritative place in the world. He would then do great things. He longed to do great things. He had not forgotten the orphanage in Korea. He had not forgotten his mission for the Lord. He would not be caught up in the negative forces of sin and vice; he would only use whatever method he had to use for stepping stones to gain the height he needed for the world to see him and listen to what he had to say.

He knew that all of the really successful actors were in most cases truly successful human beings, and he was aware that degradation and sin did not have to pave the road to stardom. But he knew they all went through the same mill, and not all of them came out unchanged. Some lost more qualities than others, and many lost all of their goodness, their values, and perhaps their souls. But he would not allow this to happen to him. He sometimes wondered a little, however, just how far one had to go for that to happen. He knew he was nearer that final loss than he cared to think; yet he could only go blindly on, following the way to stardom that he saw or that others pointed out to him.

Those who were with him spoke the loudest, and Professor Hale's letters cried out only faintly from far away. And Monica's letters, filled with love, devotion, and what money she could spare, were but faint whispers in the distant background of a clamorous, compelling orchestra.

One had to keep trying. There was no rest. One dared not lose step, and a day or two was enough to lose one's place in this hectic race to achieve the recognition of the big people in the small and frantically whirling world. So Gary dared not lose pace. He made the same efforts that other aspiring actors and actresses made and did not look back. He dared not. He felt dizzy and sick when he looked back. He must look only ahead.

He realized that the people at the agency were right and decided that since he was there to become a great movie star, he should listen to the star-makers. He listened, conformed, and began to try his best to pick up all the tricks of the trade, regardless of how little he yet knew of the trade.

Then he had a priceless chance to do a screening for a very important producer. He polished the scene until he was perfect. To his satisfaction, he gave an excellent performance before the camera. But the producer was so drunk at the time that he scarcely knew what was going on. Afterward, at the showing, he did not even know who Gary was and had abandoned the whole idea by then anyway. This was par for Hollywood, Gary, in his grieving, was told. Promises there were made to be broken.

Though endlessly broken, Gary still believed that some promises must surely sometime contain some integrity, or films would not be made, pictures finished, or actors acclaimed. And since he knew full well he had something to offer and a better background for acting and appearing before a camera or in public than most people had who were attempting and actually becoming actors in Hollywood, he was not yet ready to give up.

Night after night, he went to nightclubs, parties, and events to be seen. He attended screenings in the daytime and parties and studio premiers at night. Image was very important in Hollywood. It was vitally important. He had begun to make great sacrifices for his image. He ate dinner regularly in the most expensive restaurants, carefully hiding the agony of pinching pennies painfully in other ways.

He still felt, in spite of this—as have many others, and not only in Hollywood—that he was quite decent. It seemed to him his decency was not affected by the indecent things he did, because these things were necessary and a part of the game. Others were doing the same things also, because they found it necessary, and this did not seem at the time to register on his scale of integrity, which had considerably lowered even in the short time he had been there.

For a time, he played very well, indeed. He felt his reason for doing it justified whatever he had to do. He let nothing harm his image. That was all-important. There was an endless parade of beautiful people for whom agents, including his, held talent competitions, exhibiting their latest male or female flesh product as if the various nightclubs were open slave markets. This was almost the extent of what an agent could do, but by making most of the arrangements himself, Gary managed to appear on some TV shows, quixotically chasing exposure on his own. Though he quite frankly enjoyed being on display and flitting around to nightclubs, he found himself getting nowhere. And his money was running out.

After a while, this parade of beautiful people who had so intrigued him began to cloy, and he felt he was becoming dazed by the glare. People clamored for him to "Live, live, live!" while he was barely able to even exist. Sometimes in his desperation—because of the parts that eluded his grasp, even though he was striving with all his might to be noticed, to be chosen, to be recognized for the actor he was—he came to the point where he felt he would do anything for even the smallest part in order to gain credits.

While he felt the brass ring was almost within his grasp, especially after he had spent some time with Helen Thayler—a beautiful drama coach, America's answer to Anna Mangani, and whom he thought should have been a successful actress—still, nothing seemed to happen. She was a very good drama coach, actress, and teacher and well able to communicate her art, but she was not a well-known actress, and Gary could never understand why she was not discovered.

She had spent some time in Europe, dubbing foreign films, and was at this time rather a newcomer to Hollywood. She and Gary had found much in common and worked together, doing scene after scene for talent scouts at various studios, both always looking for the big break that was waiting for them.

It was long in coming, it seemed to Gary. Increasingly, in his moments of despair and frustration, he began to feel that the life he led was not his life—that he was not himself. He seemed possessed by some demon of desire that kept him kicking and scratching at the closed door that had seemed so ready to open on his arrival. While he was enjoying it all, in a way, especially the dates with the young and nubile beauties that abounded, he began to have a feeling of imminent disaster, even though everything seemed to be going well.

There were also times when he picked up a little money here and there. But he became panicky in proportion to his cash on hand. He felt, of course, that he could and would survive until those golden doors opened, and then everything would be wonderful, but it was very difficult to wait, survive, and keep up his image on so little.

He was still receiving many invitations to studio premiers and special screenings, and despite his own tentative departures from the straight and narrow, he felt that God's hand was guiding him all the while, and he was still only waiting for the summons to play Jesus. This would vindicate all he had been forced to do to gain a desired end. After that, he felt he would be able to give so much to the world that he would be forgiven through the souls he would save when at last his own true role in life was exposed. With the fame he would achieve as a star, the souls he could reach and save would be limitless. By this reasoning, he felt God was still guiding him in spite of all he had to do that might be despicable in the eyes of any truly faithful follower of Christ.

But he was now in a world that required a totally different point of view. And if he was ever to achieve the goal he had set his heart on, he must follow the rules of this world, however distasteful. These rules were very different from the restrictions he was accustomed to. But he could learn them, and he set about doing it with determination. He felt that he was still being careful not to step too far over the boundary line laid down by his Christian faith.

Chapter 9

Costume Ball

The Press Photographers Costume Ball burst upon the Hollywood scene like Cinderella's ball. It was the place of discovery. This was the one greatest opportunity of the year to show what you were and what you could be—to be discovered.

Gary was inspired to go as the reincarnation of Rudolph Valentino. He had not yet abandoned this idea. This would be his greatest opportunity. He had been told that he reminded people of Rudy. He had studied Rudy's life, visited his grave, and he felt he was, if not the reincarnation of the man, somehow a kindred spirit of this passionate departed god who was so mourned.

Of course, he had dates. Any good-looking man in Hollywood had dates with the ubiquitous beauties who flocked, there roaming the streets, clogging every public affair, looking for a chance to be seen with a good-looking man. And Gary was handsome. At twenty-five, suave, six foot one, he was attractive to women, and he was considered a prize to be seen with. He was, in fact, not counting the known stars, the most perfect showcase at that time for any of the eager starlets or would-be starlets to be seen with. He was popular, but he was lonely.

He was aware that he was merely being used, as he knew that he used any important person or name he could possibly, even remotely, be associated with. He, in fact, had learned to use anyone who might give him an opportunity to be discovered. This was a cardinal rule of the game. And failing in that, he would, at least, be exposed. It was all exposing. All the frantic jockeying was for the express purpose of being exposed, seen, and possibly remembered when a part came up in which he or she could be used. Using was the name of the game.

Hollywood itself was one large holding pen where talent paraded itself in glory and in shame—anything to be seen, to be noticed, to be observed. It was vital to be seen. At each public function, all the hundreds—thousands—of milling paraders were constantly on display, willing to sell their very souls at wholesale—or less. At clubs and parties, they would parade and be seen as racehorses are seen in a paddock, with onlookers pointing out this good feature, that bad feature, that one lacking the vital "if only" feature. All were watched and studied—the way they walked, talked, laughed, and did other things that were required. They were in the paddock, on display, and for sale. And all fought madly to be shown in this piece-of-meat fashion—to be judged by their definite inferiors. But this was overlooked, because those inferiors were in the superior positions of being choosers and had to be catered to. They were the buyers.

So Gary was involved in this degradation, because it was a requirement. And now he was delighted to be invited to this particular Press Photographers Costume Ball, because it would give him the chance for exposure as the great lover, Rudolph Valentino. He wanted to attend the ball in the actual sheik's costume that Rudolph Valentino had worn. But this idea was shattered when he found that it cost $200 to rent it for only a few hours. Sick at heart, he settled for a copy.

He had selected his companion for this night, one of the heartbreakingly beautiful studio secretaries—one of Mr. DeMille's secretaries, actually. She dressed as an old-time barmaid, and a lovely barmaid she was. She, as all the secretaries in that great arena, had played the game at first. But they had seen the futility before some of the others had and had taken jobs that not only supported them, but also gave them a little more dignity than the usual hangers-on among the feverish, lovely, hopeful starlets. The secretaries were not so easily impressed with famous names and could pick and choose their own dates instead of being the victims of any boor who had clawed his way to fame or partial fame.

Gary had found Arlita a delightful and beautiful companion, but knowing that this ball was an important showcase for aspiring actor's attributes, Gary soon forgot her in the absorbing interest of showing himself. All the guests at the ball were falling over each other to make an impression—any impression, good or bad, but noticeable—and doing anything at all to get their picture in the papers.

During the evening in which Gary was slowly becoming aware that almost no one had noticed the costume he was wearing or was impressed by it, a really beautiful, very young girl, virtually naked, had herself carried in by four hired "slaves." The thing Gary noticed, however, was the extra efforts the men who were the slaves, also almost naked, made to show themselves off. They took this opportunity for a double purpose, unknown to their young employer, who remained hidden until the last moment of suspense. The slaves had used the time by then to show themselves to their advantage and were desperately competing with the woman's beauty. They vigorously displayed their own beautified physical attractions, all trying to be important—to be seen. When the dazzling, unattired girl arose from her cramped and covered position, she had to attempt to tear the attention away from her own slaves, who had gotten a very good start on her.

Jeff Chandler, standing beside Gary, remarked, "What next?" in a bored tone. "If the talent isn't there," he added, "they can run naked through the streets, and it won't help." And Gary had agreed. But he was aware that talented or not, many were getting noticed, getting their names remembered, and being called for parts while he, desperately gamboling at balls, premiers, parties, screenings, and nightclubs in the hope of any part at all, was being ignored. He remembered and believed now what the top publicist at Fox Studios had told him when he had first arrived—that an axiom of that incredible society was, "Keep your name in the papers. It doesn't matter what they write about you. Just keep your name there."

He had seen, however, that not all successful actors and actresses believed that. Lauren Bacall had not. She had been so disturbed on the set of *The Gift of Love,* where she was starring with Robert Stack, that she had left the set, offended, when a rumor about her was printed in a paper. Gary still remembered her exotic perfume and felt a vast disappointment that she would not present herself to be photographed with him and Mr. Stack, who was very genial and pleasant. Mr. Stack had been very kind, and Gary was forever grateful for his help in getting him acquainted with other fine actors and actresses.

And after a while, in his struggle to serve both God and mammon, Gary conceived a sort of compromise that appeased his spiritual stress and gave him, at the same time, a showcase for his talents. In this effort, he felt inspired. He was desperately trying to find a compromise, because he could not betray his dream of reaching the world through fame somehow with at least one of his dichotomy of passions. It had become an obsession to succeed in some way in this dream world that was fast becoming a nightmare from which he even feared to awaken.

He told himself that within this new idea, he had conceived a worthy cause and was honoring the Lord in the process of furthering his own career. And this furthering did not seem wrong to him. He felt only that it had led him to the perfect vehicle for his faith and for the glorification of Christ, which he intended it to be. In some strange spiritual compromise, Gary now turned to an idea that had been gathering in his mind during sleepless nights when the liqueur he had consumed along with the coffee made him lie awake until the dawn, trying to hide from himself under the pillows, where even tears could not relieve him.

It was just too much, he eventually decided—all this showing and being exposed until the emotions were raw—and shame and humiliation had become almost normal feelings. Always, of course, there was the necessity to blame it on. But now there seemed no way he could appeal to Jesus to save him from the agony he had chosen to endure.

The sudden death of Professor Hale shocked him back to reality. He had not been prepared for that. He had felt that Professor Hale was his one rock of Gibraltar who would never falter in his love. Now Gary had no anchor. He was adrift in a sea of iniquity such as he had never dreamed of. He had always felt he was not really a part of it and could climb out and be clean at will. But now the love and faith of the one person—Professor Hale—whom he had so depended upon was suddenly gone.

In the endless grasping for a handhold on fame and fortune in a crazy madhouse with others even madder than he, if that were possible, he felt that with the passing away of this one true believer in his soul's strength, he was not bereft and truly alone. And he was shockingly not all sure of the strength of his soul. Even so, he did not ask for forgiveness; he asked for strength to go on. He begged anew for the big break. And then he found himself pleading for just a break. But nothing came of anything he did.

The thought at last had begun to swirl around in his brain that perhaps he was not going to be helped to do this thing he so desired to do. Perhaps there was some other way he was supposed to go. And after thinking about this, he allowed thoughts to come and go concerning another idea.

This idea was new. It was a concept for a one-man show with himself as the hero. He needed a showcase. What better showcase for his special talents than in a play—a play whereby he might honor the Lord in the process. He felt that somehow he must find his way back, and he had found himself feeling utterly alone since the death of Dr. Hale.

Was this new idea a way out of his dilemma of being a nonentity in a teeming sea of frenetic nonentities? He began to put his mind to work, thinking seriously about this new idea and picturing it in his mind. It was novel, but it seemed attractive, and it might be possible.

Chapter 10

Young Finnish Actor

"I CAN BUILD A BRIDGE TO my Lord's approval," muttered Gary to himself. Perhaps, he thought, Professor Hale, now with the Lord, was approving of this. He did not dare ask God's approval at this point. He felt he would have to redeem himself somehow in some way before he dared to face his Maker, even in his mind. And he determined to make this new concept a bridge back to his Lord's approval, from which he had strayed so terrifyingly far. His spirits rose as he thought of this new inspiration, and he was determined now to try to present a show of his own.

This show would consist mainly of a dramatic reading of the great story of Jesus, and if he could not yet play Christ in *The Greatest Story* on the screen, he could certainly do the reading he had in mind on the stage with conviction. He would use his resounding voice in a reading of the life of Christ, which he would himself prepare, and in his sincerity, he would bring Christ to earth—to the people. Those who came to hear his play would go away inspired and would tell their friends of this new one-man show he would deliver. The setting he chose was the Hollywood Center Theatre, and he'd call his show *The Weeping King*.

It was a great thrill to see his name up on the billboards, as he had hoped to see it one day. Now he was proud and happy and felt he was at last on the road to success. He was determined to achieve success in one way or another, and he felt certain that this showing of his talent would convince that right people whom he needed to attract.

On opening night, when he proudly walked out on stage, he was aware of only one thing—people were watching him, and he was exactly where he belonged. It was a thrilling moment, and he felt an added dimension of pride, because he was honoring the Lord. He felt good, and his performance was good. And if the applause was thin, he didn't notice. In his mind, he saw a vast audience—a totally different audience from the real one. He saw an audience of the future.

It was like a dream come true for Gary to be here before an audience. It was just as well for him that his eyes were blinded by the footlights and the zeal with which he sought his goal, for the audience would not have satisfied him otherwise. But Gary knew he gave the performance of his life each time he read his play, and he kept seeing Professor Hale's smiling face out there across the footlights that mercifully shielded him from the scattered faces floating sparsely beyond their dazzling glare.

He could see in his mind the seats packed. He saw every eye upon him. He saw his friends and relatives, his father and his mother, and his sister in the audience out there, smiling with approval. Monica was there. All those he loved were there. He played to them and to his beloved Christ, whom he felt he had betrayed in times of crisis and in time of need. Now he felt forgiven—or at least, not so forsaken. And with hopeful heart, he did his very best.

He also did his best, because he counted on this show to impress the powers of Hollywood—to remind them that he had come there to play the part of Christ in *The Greatest Story* and that he was the best choice for the portrayal. His play, he felt, would surely convince the moguls of the industry that he, of all those in Hollywood aspiring to do the part, would be the best possible actor to depict the character of Christ. His own stage production would prove it.

But the news from Twentieth Century-Fox was discouraging. *The Greatest Story* seemed to be making no progress at all.

People came to see him. They did not actually break the doors down or crowd the theater. But they came, and many saw his show. He was talked about, and he received good reviews from several columnists. One very good review was written by Russell Tate of the *Hollywood Diary,* which said, "Mr. Heikkila, himself, displays a magnificently resonant voice, flawless diction, a great deal of personal charm and talent. He could develop into a fine addition to the ranks of any film company."

Gary was thrilled with this and expected at any time to be called to special screenings or to receive some response from those in power in Hollywood. They could not ignore him now, he felt certain. He lived on hope and existed only for the next performance.

The several notable critical writings he got also cheered him greatly, since the columnist, Jane Wooster, had taken in his show. In one of her columns, she commented, "Gary Heikkila, exciting young Finnish actor, was considered the Sir Laurence Olivier of the pulpit long before this self-imposed exile left the clergy for Celluloidia..." Now, they could not but pay attention, he felt, and expected to hear from the powers-that-be-now.

But time went by, and the news about *The Greatest Story,* which he had still hoped to be chosen for, was that it was being sold to George Stevens. And it was said that the Swedish actor Max Von Sydow would be chosen by him to play the part of Christ. Now there was no more hope of getting the part that had brought him to Hollywood.

Gary was crushed beyond measure, but his show continued. And while he still attracted a certain class of people, he did not attract the numbers he hoped for or the particular people he needed to get him into the film world as an actor of merit. The audience dwindled away as time passed, and his best efforts went unrewarded. Finally, he realized he would have to close his show.

When he gave his last performance, he felt an exhaustion he had not felt since his depression at the end of the way in Korea. This was the same, in a way. He felt sick and defeated, and he was devastated not only by the closing of his show, but also by having had no response to his performance from the sources he had hoped to attract. But mostly, his depression sprang from his role in *The Greatest Story* having been given by now to someone else. He felt this was a bitter betrayal.

He had waited so long. He was not only devastated, but also broke—stone broke, with nowhere to turn. How could he play any part or obtain any part if he could not eat and had no place to sleep? This was a desperate situation. Good friends, buddies, and even his true friends, he found, were too busy with still being exposed to give him any time, much less help him to make enough money to live on.

He was truly in a bind. An actor did not work. An actor did not wash dishes or park cars. He was an actor, after all, and he must keep his image—the image of Garrison Gray—untarnished. And though he was temporarily in a slack period, he was still an actor, and a successful actor did not need to take a job. To do so would fatally reveal a lack of success. It was imperative to look successful.

No money had dribbled in from Monica or from home for some time, and he could not ask for any. He had to find a cheaper place to live, though he did not know where it would be. And he also had to pretend he was doing all right. He simply had to get back into the Hollywood swing of seeking exposure, because he had to get some small parts, and by this method, he could climb up. Then, after that, everyone would see that he really had been right to come to Hollywood and had become a great movie star after all. He would show them all that he could to it. It was only a matter of time. But in the meantime, he had to keep on pretending, as everyone in Hollywood did; he had to hang on with teeth and toenails and still keep up a front.

But he couldn't stay at the small apartment he had rented any longer. Where could he go? With almost his last cent, he rented a tiny, cheap hotel room of the type called a flop on a street called Hope in lower Los Angeles. It was even further downtown than the YMCA. There was no glamour on Hope Street. There was no glamour in all of downtown Los Angeles, and it was a long way from Hollywood's Sunset and Vine.

Gary still managed to get to Hollywood. He didn't feel the need to tell anyone there that he had moved, so for a while, he scrabbled a little here and there and managed to make the rounds of being exposed and then made his way back to his scrubby little room on Hope Street. Living in Hollywood was completely out of the question. He looked at the peeling paint on the walls of his room and slept on the worn-out bed night after night without a glimmer of a chance in any of the studios, and still he would not give up.

Gary Heikkila, recently photographed by Alphonse Micciche, PPA Master of Photography, Samuels Studio, Maynard, Massachusetts.

Dr. Heikkila photographed with Pat Boone in Pat's Beverly Hills home.

20th Century-Fox photo (1957) of Gary Heikkila as the Christ in a test for the proposed major film The Greatest Story Ever Told. The film was never made by Fox.

Gary Heikkila poses with film actress, Zsa Zsa Gabor, in her Beverly Hills mansion.

Gary did a one-man show (a reading) entitled The Weeping King at the Hollywood Center Theatre in Hollywood.

Gary Heikkila plays a minister in a scene from Otto Preminger's "Tell Me You Love Me, Junie" with Lisa Minnelli and the late actor James Coco.

Gary Heikkila appears in Otto Preminger's "Tell Me You Love Me, Junie Moon" with Liza Minnelli and the late James Coco. This Paramount Pictures film was released in 1970.

Heikkila was 29 when he left Hollywood, the week Marilyn Monroe died, 1962, speaks at the Grace Evangelical Free Church in Gardner, MA.

Dr. Heikkila speaks at the Harvard Memorial Church, Harvard University, at a special memorial service for the late Dr. Mildred Fay Jefferson. She was the first black woman to graduate from the Harvard Medical School. Heikkila joined other distinguished personalities to honor this renowned founder of the Right to Life movement.

Then one day, great excitement came to the ancient little hotel. A Spanish movie producer had called Gary's room. The hotel, filled mostly with young dishwashers and waitresses, old men and women, drunks, and down-at-the-heel salesmen, rang with the importance of this news. It had spread quickly from the hotel desk in the lobby, and Garrison Gray was suddenly a celebrity. They had known it all along, they told each other.

The producer had come to Hollywood from Spain to get backing for his production of a story about Christ. He was also casting for the main character, and since Gary was well-known as having been considered for the part of Christ in *The Greatest Story*, the producer had heard of this and called his hotel, asking to meet him.

Gary was in no shape to meet a producer that morning when he received the call. He answered it from the battered wall phone in the hall. He was near to fainting at the brusque announcement that this big man from Spain would be right out to see him.

Hardly in shape to impress a producer, Gary was stunned. He had about run out of the stuff one gets excited with, and he could only think dismally, *here comes another broken promise.* He almost went back to bed and to sleep. Hope springs eternal in the human breast, it is said, and Gary was still at least that human.

A crashing knock came on the flimsy panels of his door. The short, stout, grizzled man, having ignored the desk clerk, stepped in with complete self-assurance when Gary opened the door to his dark den of a room.

Gary had just allowed the thought to pass through his mind that maybe opportunity would open its mysterious door to a whole new world for him as he now closed the door behind his visitor. And then when he turned to the man, he knew it would be a difficult interview.

This producer was even cruder than the usual Hollywood producers who size up an actor or actress like a side of beef, and the familiar sensation of having no human dignity at all came back to Gary at once. The talent parades had been no worse, surely, than the close scrutiny that he was now enduring under such adverse conditions.

This short, balding producer had boldly walked a step or two across the miserable room and rolled up the shade, letting in the shockingly brazen Los Angeles sunlight. It was like a torch lighting up the squalid room in all its littered shabbiness and shame. This indeed was the very bottom rung of the ladder of humility for Gary. And this brazen man could not help but see it in the glare he had deliberately and callously created. He motioned Gary over to the window, and studied his face closely.

Gary was so self-conscious in these embarrassing surroundings while the director impassively scrutinized his countenance that he was almost tempted to fall on his knees and plead and beg for a break, a small part, any kind. And in the following interval, he wasn't quite sure whether in another moment of this silent scrutiny he would have been able to refrain from being defensive, compulsively contending he was truly a great actor, merely slumming here for a lark, hiding, resting up from the hectic life of constant acting. Or he might have come out with the bitter truth—that he was an utterly washed up actor before he had even gotten started.

And then, just at the breaking point, when he was ready to babble or confess all—anything to break the dreadful silence—the director began to talk and relieved the tension. He pontifically explained his motive for the film, which seemed good, and revealed some of the ideas, and Gary began to relax. This man seemed sincere. Maybe. Perhaps … just maybe …

Nothing was concluded, but the director did seem interested in Gary, and by the time he left, Gary had regained his ability to cope and even to hope. He prayed a most earnest little prayer after the door closed behind the producer, ending it with, "Dear God, if this is the way, I'm ready! Oh, I am ready!"

Chapter 11

A Supernatural Intervention

Ready, Gary waited, and he waited. And he never heard a word. Days and then weeks went by.

Too disillusioned to be bitter, he simply kept plugging along. He had been up and down the street too long to let disappointment affect him greatly. Hollywood, he had come to believe, was just one huge broken promise. Promises meant no more there than a smile from a waitress. It was a part of the business to make promises. You were supposed to know that; and after a while, you did.

He still went to Hollywood, but going back there day after day from that shabby little room was wearing him to a threadbare shadow of his former self. He read *Variety* and the *Hollywood Reporter,* keeping up with the films proposed to be made. He hustled to every audition or screening where he thought he might be even vaguely suited to the part and even to those he knew were hopeless. It was something to do.

He was everywhere. He knew all the tricks now. He even knew the game. He played it. He was becoming an old-timer, and he knew he would surely be recognized soon. He was an actor. He had proved that with his own production, and he had proved it at TV appearances, parties, and many screenings. And on top of that, he had learned to make light jokes, act rich and comfortable at nightclubs, and carry on the light social banter typical of these gatherings. He had to compete with the multitudes of other would-be's on all sides and to try simultaneously to impress the important big shots who were there. He did that, and he did it well.

He did everything he was supposed to do. Why couldn't they recognize what a great actor he was? Why couldn't they see how dedicated he was to the game of acting—to the game of Hollywood? Why were they so blind to his efforts, potential, and abilities? What did it take? He was doing everything right, he knew. He had learned in the year that he had been there what was right and what was wrong. He could not bear to be among the great majority who came and did not conquer—those who went home defeated.

In this turbid atmosphere, he was able to see that sin was a harsh taskmaster, brutal and unmerciful in its demands, driving the victim in a relentless downward path subtly, robbing him of all he held sacred in his heart. Spiritually slipped away, and life became geared to the satisfactions possible in an impoverished state while a person was still sentient enough to be alive. And merely being alive became the basic problem; the entrapment was not to be broken and held many in its murky toils to the end.

Gary, feeling nothing, yet rebelled. Something within him would not be conquered. He was about to be lost, but he would not be willingly lost. And if lost, he knew that no one needed to stay lost. But how would he get back to the fold? He agonized. Oh, how far he had strayed—too far, he feared. Perhaps he could not return now even if he wanted to. But did he really want to? He searched his soul and found it in dire pain.

In his hard and narrow bed, he searched his heart for the truth of what he really wanted—what really held him there. Yes, he had come there to play the part of Christ, but could he play that part truthfully now? He had come there to serve the Lord. Was he serving the Lord?

No, he had to confess. Underneath it all—all the glorious pretense of a purpose—he must have really wanted to pretend; perhaps he loved pretense. Perhaps that was why he loved the movies. He had really wanted to be a big movie star, and perhaps he was only using his desire to spread the Word of Jesus for an excuse. Was he pretending? And what was he pretending? Was he pretending to himself? Had he pretended all along? How despicable. He hated himself if this was true. He denied it. It could not be true.

Yet in the morning, he again made his way back by bus to Hollywood, admitting nothing, still not sure of his motives, but unable to truly examine them. It was too painful. Each day, he joined the crowd of hangers-on and spent the balance of the day and half the night in the usual way. Then, back on Hope Street, nor far from Skid Row in downtown Los Angeles, he slept until it was nearly noon. And then one day, he could not make himself go back to Hollywood anymore.

All his reasons were gone. What good would it do? It would only drag him further down the ladder of degradation. It would destroy him. Why was he doing this? He asked himself this. This was not his life. It would never be his life. He had lived a practically monastic life even throughout the war.

He had been an assistant chaplain. Then there were the years afterward in the Temple Schools, where he was proud to be himself. But here in this strange setting, he dared not let the real Gary Heikkila emerge. He must hide his calling, background, and real identity. As Garrison Gray, he was denying everything that was real. He was living a lie. But perhaps he belonged here in pretend land with the other pretenders. Maybe he was one of them. Yet his soul cried out, denying this. But what could he do that was honorable while staying there? He could not admit his identity. Who would want to crash a party with a gospel minister?

He was trapped in pretense. But he told himself he had asked for it. He had wanted to pretend—and pretend he had. Yet was not all acting pretending? He justified himself with this thought. Pretending to others was one thing, he suddenly realized in a flash of lucidity; pretending to oneself was another. He faced harsh reality as he had never faced it before. In pain, he made his decision. He would still pretend for a fee as an actor, but he would not keep pretending for free, on display, in the hope of being discovered.

Surely God would not desert him, even though he knew he had deserted God in his selfish interests and in his need. God had forgiven others; God would forgive him. He had always felt certain of that. But Gary also knew the conditions of forgiveness.

"Go and sin no more," were the terms. Christ had told them this when He had lived on earth. And Christ was God's son. He had told the world of God's ways, and God's instructions for living decently were also in the Holy Bible.

At that moment, Gary saw the church. It was just a little church, and he saw it suddenly. He had never seen that church before on Hope Street. His feet dragged as he walked along, trying to think. He realized now that he had turned off Hope Street into a narrow side street and had wandered quite a way down it, and there was a church standing there before him.

He had been praying for one. Was he dreaming? He looked at the closed door. It looked real. But of course, in the middle of the morning, it would be locked; he was certain of that.

Still, an impulse drove him up the narrow wooden steps to the door. It was a little white clapboard church, standing in a rather forlorn barren yard with spots of wilted grass, and the paint was not too new. He tried the door without thinking. It opened to his touch. Strangely, it was not locked.

Then there would certainly be someone in it—maybe the minister, who could pray with him. God would surely forgive him if He knew how repentant he was and how firm his mind was now against the sins, however large or small, he had committed. He would truly "go and sin no more."

But the little church was empty. It was dark and filled with seats. Still, he knelt in the back, poured his heart out in tearful whispers in the silent church, and wept more tears than he knew he had.

As he dried his eyes at last, he saw a door. He tried the door and found that it led to a stairway. Maybe he could seek help from someone, he thought, with his knees trembling, and he started down the steps. He knew he was in need of help.

He went down the steps cautiously, finding they led to a basement that was empty except for three long trestle tables set up for a church supper that would probably be held that night, he thought. Desperately, he searched for food. Then he saw the tables were bare, and so was the small kitchen when he went through the swinging door and searched. No food anywhere. They would probably bring the food with them that night.

God—oh, dear God. What had happened to his mission—his mission for the Lord, his call that he had not answered for all these months of trying to win fame in Hollywood so that he could reach more people? He hadn't forgotten his calling; he knew this in his heart. He had just put it aside to pick up later at a more opportune time. That was all. Could God understand that?

He imagined he saw a small crust of bread lying beside the plate he had pushed aside to lay his head down. He was hallucinating. There was no food. How could there be? Where had it come from?

But he thought no more of that. He snatched up the crust before it disappeared and began to chew it. It tasked so delicious that he was tempted to swallow it all at once, but he restrained himself. He savored that hard, dry crust of bread, and it tasted better than any delicious meal he had ever eaten. It was real, and it was filling. When he had chewed it very slowly and had eaten the last crumb, he felt fulfilled. He also felt a rising of his spirits and knew that somehow, he had received an answer. He was forgiven. He felt it. Gary felt this to be a supernatural intervention of a loving, sympathetic, compassionate, and forgiving Lord God Christ.

He knelt then and thanked his Lord Jesus with tears flooding his face, which was lifted joyfully to heaven. He understood anew the truth of Matthew 4:4: "Men shall not live by bread alone." He had seen the face of vice, and it was ugly—so repulsive he would not gaze upon it again for fame or fortune.

Back at the hotel on Hope Street, he opened his mailbox with a deep sigh and took out a letter. Slowly he turned it over and saw that it was from Monica. He hadn't been fair with Monica either, he told himself, turning the letter over and over in his hand as he went back to his room.

He felt very sleepy—totally exhausted—and he wanted nothing but to crawl into his unmade bed and go to sleep. "She couldn't forgive me," he concluded, remembering her last few letters. So he would not open Monica's letter.

He crawled into bed and covered himself up. He then realized he was in his clothes, and it was hot, but he was too tired to care. He had propped Monica's letter up on the scarred little dresser, and the small pale blue envelope seemed to stand there, crying out to him, making him see Monica's face, so he turned away.

But he couldn't sleep. As he got up slowly and tiredly, he reached across to the dresser, got Monica's letter, and opened it. A check for $100 tumbled out of it and fluttered to the floor.

Chapter 12

June and Charlotte

Gary wept with joy. Then he dressed in his other suit and walked to the only bank where he was known well enough to cash an out-of-town check. As soon as he had the money in his pocket, he went to a restaurant.

The money would not last long at this rate, he knew. He had to face the truth realistically, and he did. He had to get a job. He took the first one offered—as a movie theater usher at the Melrose Theater in downtown Los Angeles. He had written to thank Monica, and he would repay her as soon as he could. She had literally saved his life.

Now he worked at what he felt was an honorable job, and while he was there, he met one of the few female theater managers in Los Angeles. She owned and managed the Paramount Theater. Within a short time, Gary was engaged there in downtown Los Angeles and began to learn the bookkeeping involved in management under Merry Hanson. A middle-aged woman who understood what he had been through, she treated him with respect and kindness, trusted him, helped him, and had confidence in him. There began to be promotions, and he became bookkeeper for the theater.

Merry was a Christlike human being. A lovely, mature woman who had been converted to Judaism, she had a firm and enduring love for people. She heard Gary's confessions out with infinite patience and helped him to know he could handle a responsible position in the business world. Gradually, he lost the terrible, burning desire for stardom and became a functioning member of society in the theater management world.

He moved from his shabby hotel room to a pleasant little apartment in Hollywood, around the corner from the Paramount Theater. Small, excellent cafes abounded nearby, and he also often dined at the attractive and popular Nichodell's restaurant, where he still saw many of his friends of studio days, when he had so frantically been searching for a part to play in movieland. Now he frequently ran into Katherine Hepburn, Lucille Ball, Tony Perkins, Sophia Loren, and other performers he knew, as well as Cecil B. Demille, the well-known director, and other far-famed personalities. The places where he met the people he admired and felt at ease with were pleasurable to Gary, even though he was now in the other end of the Hollywood productions. He was still in the theatrical world he enjoyed and in touch with his friends, but now he was earning a respectable salary.

Monica Evans had begged him to return home in the letter with the blessed $100 check. And she had told him in that letter and many more that followed that she could not wait forever. She has wanted more than anything in the world, she said, to see him in *The Greatest Story Ever Told,* but since that was done, why would he not come back to his calling? Had he not had enough of Hollywood?

There had been others, Monica knew, but she never mentioned them. June and Charlotte were both married, and she was still waiting, but she more than hinted that she could not wait forever. He knew he should give up, but now he felt he had nowhere else to turn. He had lost his dear friend and mentor, Professor Hale, in death. He had not felt the call for years, and he was well-established in business.

He could not even reveal his true calling as ordained minister to these hedonistic Hollywood devotees. They would laugh him out of town. He was still trapped in this assumed personality of the romantic lead, and outside his business, his name was still the more appealing Garrison Gray. He could not say, "I am a minister." And even though Billy Graham ministered to Judy Garland and there were many more in Hollywood who did believe, there were more who did not. Pat Boone, himself a Christian, had said to Gary, "I would never encourage a Christian to go into show business, because it's such an ego trip."

Gary had not applied that to himself. He was not on an ego trip. He still felt he had a purpose and that he could not desert it. He was still in the midst of Hollywood and could be discovered at any moment. His dream could yet come true. And he had lost his place anywhere else by now. But sometimes he felt himself emerging from the hopelessness of his Hollywood dream. And at those times, he felt he was on his way back to the living. Slowly, his call began to come back, though he did not welcome it and felt only confused.

It vanished under the shock of Monica's writing to tell him she was marrying someone else. He could not believe it. Here he was, working hard at a mundane job of a lifetime when he had lost the part of playing Jesus in *The Greatest Story,* and Monica would not even wait for him. He had talked with his friend, Merry Hanson, the beautiful-souled, blonde, handsomely coiffured businesswoman who was wise in the ways of the world. She offered him sympathy and added work. It was what he needed.

She told him he seemed to have something about him that made people like him and believe in him. He had not really been aware of it. But now he began to see it, because although he had concealed even what was left of his relationship with the Lord, people seemed to come to him with their spiritual problems. One had been a young Italian man who had lately come to Hollywood with similar ideas to his when he had first arrived. Gary found Roger Walsh almost destitute, asking for a job, and had helped him and given him knowledgeable counsel about Hollywood.

Roger profited from this and had turned away in time, and gradually, Gary began to have some kind of trust in his own faith again. His faith had never really left him, of course, but he had felt that in his forsaking God, God had forsaken him. Of course, this was not so. God never forsakes anyone, he came to realize, but he still felt he deserved to be punished, and like so many who did not understand cause and effect, he could not leave the effect to nature but felt he should be punished. So he began to punish himself under the pretext that God was doing it.

This led him into a deep depression, and had he not been able to unburden himself to Merry, he might never have recovered. But he did recover, and incredibly, even to himself, he realized he was still looking for his big break in the movies.

It was at this time that Paramount Theater was sold, razed, and replaced by a large and beautiful Bank of America building. But Merry had assured Gary of a good position in another chain of theaters. He was using well the teaching she had invested in him during his initial difficulty with theater bookkeeping. Soon he was executive manager of two Paramount theaters in downtown Los Angeles—both the Roxy and the Arcade—with all the responsibilities of administrative powers.

Gary still lived in Hollywood. It had been nearly four years since his arrival in fantasyland. But no big break in the movies had come, and one day, he looked at himself in the mirror and asked if he was crazy. "Maybe," he answered himself, and he went on looking for a break. He couldn't stop hoping and believing his big break would still come. But he was a professional businessman now and had been for the past two years. With Merry, he had learned theater management and could get work anywhere. He laughed at himself, but he knew that he was still hoping.

But finally, the inevitable day came when he realized he no longer needed to hope. He had found satisfaction in being what he was. It was time to admit that his big break was not going to come; it was not meant to be. He was a businessman and was probably never going to be an outstanding star in the movies. This did not shake him as it once would have done. He could accept it. Lots of worthwhile and successful people had never been movie stars. He realized he would not have wanted to pay the price, now that he knew what it was, had he won stardom. But still, he could not leave the world of movies. He could not entirely let go of his dream. He had had it too long.

He began to realize then, as he had sensed once before, that he must have a dual personality. One part of him was dedicated to the theatrical world—the land of glamour, glory, and glitter. It had always been. He loved it. He loved this tinsel world. He felt a natural part of it. He loved the people. He knew many stars personally and enjoyed being with them. He loved the movieland talk—the show business talk, the banter. He loved the open, generous, large-hearted nature of show people—knowledgeable, kind, loving, forgiving, tolerant, petty, envious, jealous, though they were at times—and he admired their marvelous courage.

He admired Zsa Zsa Gabor and had pictures taken with her in her Bel Air mansion. Her nerve and vivaciousness—the same off screen as on—truly enamored him. She was very pleasant to be with and fun to know. Others he also liked, and he saw the kindness and fine generosity of their natures.

Perhaps he felt guilty, because he found himself still dreaming in his heart of Hollywood as his vehicle to spread the word of Christ throughout the land. He still longed to be a success in Hollywood. What a witness Hollywood could be to the rest of the world. If Christ could get a foothold there, he often thought, how far might he then spread God's wonderful Word? The talent and the technicians that could be put to work for the Lord would surely affect an enormous influence on the rest of the world. No doubt, if Christ came to earth that day, He would use the marvelous advantages of movies to reach a fascinated, watching world.

But the other side of Gary argued with this. Those people were not ready yet. They were too far from the spiritual world of Christ. It was hopeless to try to win them to Christ—even more hopeless than to hope for one's own break in Hollywood. He asked himself, *Are your own spiritual powers strong enough to overcome what you have seen in Hollywood? Are you a Don Quixote, breaking your sword on windmills? Do what you can, but find more fertile ground than this. You cannot make a dent in Hollywood.* But it was hard for him to give up trying.

Chapter 13

THE REAL GARY HEIKKILA

"WHAT AM I DOING AS a businessman in Los Angeles?" asked Gary, disgruntled. Was this what God had intended for him? He was an ordained minister. Was he to hide away like this forever? Had God not forgiven him? Could he not forgive himself? Could he not now go where he could be more himself? His other personality—the strong one—was slowly reasserting itself. Suddenly, he felt as out of place in the business world as he had in Hollywood.

This life, he realized, was so far from his own true life he led before he had come to Hollywood that when this nature began to emerge again, Gary was stunned. He did not know himself. It was hard to believe he had thought he could lead this life, which was merely an offshoot of Hollywood and kept him in touch with it. But that was a good life. It was an honest and clean life. And being a businessman pleased him. Why did he feel a pull in another direction—back to God's work? What was he to people? He was two entirely different kinds of people. Which was the real Gary Heikkila?

Was he the romantic Garrison Gray, the handsome movie actor, who settled for a business life in the midst of glamour, vending it, to be part of it at least, still waiting to be discovered, or was he Gary Heikkila, the devoted follower of Jesus—the disciple, the minister, the man of God who had been wayward and sinned but had been forgiven and now wanted nothing more than to spread the word of Christ in his own small way? Perhaps he was still in his heart the glamorous movie star he had hoped to be, converting the world to Jesus through his own fame and world-renowned leadership in a world of fantasy-making. Emerging from stardom gained in a different world, would not his wealth and fame then allow him to utilize all of Hollywood's most wonderful and commanding facilities? His other personality persisted in asking this.

Could he really ever be content in a smaller world, to do his little bit? This personality argued with him. *Yes. No.* The answers seemed to come, only to confuse him more. "Who am I?" he asked desperately, hoping God would tell him. "Who is the real me?" he pleaded to be told.

Only a small, still voice inside him answered with a question. *Who do you want to be?*

"Oh, dear God, help me," Gary cried in anguish. "I truly do not know!"

But you are the one who must decide, the small, still voice insisted. *You cannot be both. You see what happens. If you try to be both, you will always fail. You will be no one. Many people are ineffective in this life, because they have never made their decision. You must decide. You must choose.*

"I can't! I can't! I don't know what to choose."

You know, the small, still voice answered. *Do you really want to stay in Hollywood? Are you going back to the exposure of nightclubs and screenings and getting into the swing again, as you have been thinking of lately? Otherwise, why are you still here? You know you have to do that to achieve your purpose there.*

"No. No, I'm not going back. I hate that life."

First, are you going to be a businessman in a business world?

"I don't know. But it has become my life."

If you are, remember this, the little voice said. *It takes all of your life. You can't stand still in the business world. You must either grow or lose your business. And do you like business practices enough to be a businessman all of your life—to involve yourself totally in business? Is that what you want from life?*

"I don't think so."

Will you make the other choice? Are you going back to your work in ministry with the full approval of God and carrying out your life's work of being a minister, which was the life you once chose?

"I'd love to, but I can't."

You have chosen, the small voice said, and it was still.

But Gary did not feel that he had chosen. He was torn and frustrated. He writhed in indecision until his forehead was wet with sweat. He could not cut himself in two and do both, could he? He'd like to. He couldn't really give up either one. But in his heart, he knew he had given up his calling long ago for his Hollywood venture. Now could he give up his Hollywood hopes and dreams and go back to his calling? Was the call strong enough? Was he truly needed to do the Lord's work in another way—a smaller, different, more personal way?

He listened for the still, small voice, but it seemed to be gone. He did not know in his agony that all human beings have the same struggle he was having against the two forces that are born within every human soul—that all humans are dual. There is no way to avoid the struggle, because human beings, unique in this world, must struggle continually to choose between the good, spiritual, positive part of their natures and the weaker, negative, human part, which is mundane and will lead them away from God—with the Devil, it may be, to the brink of hell and beyond, if one will follow. All are born with a two-sided nature. Free will alone allows us to choose the side we wish to follow.

God is so forgiving that we may follow the bad to the very edge of hell, and He will take us back into his heart, love us, receive us with our wounds, and heal us. And though Gary knew this, the myriad thoughts, fears, doubts, and questions that beset all mankind were in his mind. He tossed and turned in an agony of doubt and indecision.

Could he give up the part of him that wanted to follow the path to stardom? *No,* he decided. *But I will be more careful now. I will not let myself fall into iniquity. I will keep above that. I will follow the path to stardom and not lose my integrity … I have learned.*

He had to stop. He knew better. He would not have the time to do this and still make a living in the business world. There was no way for him to win in this game of chasing fame that requires the underdog to cater to the upper dog. He had become aware of what the game was. This could never be a fair game. Christ warned us of this game. It was the publican's game. But in Hollywood, the game must be played by all; whether one lost or won, one had to compete in any way one could. The winners today could lose tomorrow. The game was endless and never over. And the sole object of the game was pure and simple—power.

Gary wondered if it was worth it. His face flushed, and he beat his pillow. He would go to sleep, and maybe he could figure it out tomorrow. He slept, worked, and wrestled with his two sides—his two personalities—and still, the answer did not come. He could not give up Hollywood, and though he knew there was nothing there for him, he still had the hope in his heart that maybe … He had so much to offer. And the rewards were so great.

But he knew now what it involved to make that dream come true, and even then, perhaps it would not come true. He would have to keep on doing what he had to do—what everyone had to do—to make it to the top in Hollywood. He was not different. There was only one road. They all traveled that road. The only difference was that some made it to the top, and others didn't. Not all could make it to the top; there wasn't room up there. And at the top, you still had to scratch and claw to stay there. Did he want that?

He already knew that business would not fulfill his heart or his talent. He was a gifted speaker. He had a remarkable voice. No matter how successful he was in business, this gift would be lost. There was no need for it. His resonant stage voice would be wasted in petty bickering and bargaining. Did he want that? Did money mean that much to him?

Did he want to waste a God-given talent? Would being in business accomplish something worthwhile? Was it something others could not do as well? Was that all the life he wanted to live? Should he let his special talents die? Was this the life God had planned for him and had given him talents for? If so, why had God called him in the first place?

Was he supposed to wear his life away, waiting for the chance to be famous so he could influence millions while there were hundreds in small churches who longed to hear the Word of God? Should he deny them because he could not reach a multitude? This question aroused a great writhing in Gary's heart. He knew he was getting close to a choice, and it was a difficult one to have to make, but he knew he had to make a decision. He knew he would have to make it, because he could find no peace between the battling elements in his mind. But he was fortunate in knowing that help was at hand. It always is, even while so few call on it.

Gary called on God to help—to make his decision. As for all humanity, there was help to be had in making the right decision. One needs only to pray sincerely and follow what one feels deeply is truly right for him or her. There is always a dominant side in everyone, and help comes when it is sincerely asked for.

Those who make the wrong decisions never know that help was there for the right decision. They gave up too soon, but the help was always there. And wrong decisions have an automatic cause and effect, as do right decisions.

Gary based his decision on what he felt deep within his soul was right for him. He could not turn away from what his deepest inner heart desired. He searched his soul and found his Hollywood ambition a camouflage for personal acclaim. But this was not entirely selfish; it had also contained a real and sincere desire to serve his Lord Jesus. He knew that. He had not meant to depart from that purpose. It was only that he had wished to depart from the tedious route he had been on in his ministerial life. He had wished to reach a larger goal through a more exciting avenue. But now he saw the error of this means. It would only inevitably lead him away from Jesus and frustrate his purpose.

Now that the way was gone, he knew he would welcome back that slow and prudent path of service to the Lord's flock. He saw that in his digression, he had surely lost his way. He deeply repented his waywardness now and felt a deep sense of loss. He knew he had brought this upon himself. But when he had humbly confessed this to the Lord, he felt a surge of strength and a feeling of rightness he would never willingly depart from again. He knew that somehow, his decision had been made.

Gary found that he wonderfully possessed the marvelous strength of character to face these bitter facts and to know himself. Knowledge, he found, can be hidden, but it cannot be reversed. So once he knew the decision had to be made for God he rejoiced in his heart, he knew the battle was over for him, though he was afraid he had lost by awakening too late. But now Gary felt that he was ready, if God was willing, to come back from the wilderness. He knew now he wanted to come back to the fold. It was now early in 1961. He had been away for four years.

He wrestled with his soul over what to do, and finally, he was inspired to take a first, tentative step. He wrote to Dr. Roberson back at Tennessee Temple, explaining much and telling him that he was ready now to honor his calling. Gary even tried to tell him why. But he waited with little hope of an understanding reply.

Dr. Roberson understood. The next week, Gary was amazed to see an article about himself in the official church paper of the Highland Park Baptist Church in Chattanooga, Tennessee when a copy was sent to him by Dr. Roberson. It stated that Rev. Gary Heikkila was available for speaking engagements.

The paper was circulated all over the country. Gary was proud, happy, and grateful. He knew he was ready for anything that would happen. There might be no response. He was even prepared for that. He thanked God for the faith Dr. Roberson had in him. That good man of God hadn't needed to hear any repentance or solid testimony to have faith in him. He had simply believed what Gary said.

The article brought immediate results. The Lord was intending to remove him really far from Hollywood, he thought, as the first letter came from Maine, where a pastor invited him to come to speak in his church. But that was out of the question. Gary did not have that much money put away. He could not begin to pay his plane fare for a nearly three thousand-mile trip and perhaps back again, and he would certainly not travel by bus, he told himself. So Gary wrote and explained and thanked the minister for the invitation.

By return mail, he was informed about the New England Fellowship of Evangelicals, whose business it was to recommend and pay for speakers' tours in their area. It was suggested that Gary get in touch with them. Gary immediately began a correspondence with Rev. Charles Campbell, the executive director of the fellowship. He was most encouraging and wrote to Dr. Roberson at once for Gary's references.

The tour was arranged for Gary to speak at all of the small New England churches specified on a long circuit, with this first stop in Boston. Gary had a wonderful feeling of purpose. Instead of the resignation to fate he would have felt had he followed the Hollywood beacon or stayed in business in Los Angeles, he could attend a marvelous command performance for the Lord. But first, he had to resign himself to traveling by bus, since that is what the fellowship offered in the way of transportation, and they would not be pleased to have it rejected.

In May of 1961, he said goodbye almost joyfully to Hollywood and to Los Angeles, knowing his choice had been made for good—and forever. He had no regrets, and he knew that while his mind had guided him afar, he had really made his choice deep in his heart long ago, and it was the right one for him.

His friends and coworkers were genuinely sorry to see him go. They tried to encourage him to stay, but even a good part in a picture now would not have persuaded him to stay. He was going back to his own reality, and he knew at last, with peace in his heart, what his reality was.

Chapter 14

Religious Superstar

"I'VE GOT TO HAVE SOME rest," Gary mumbled. Gary's heart was at peace; however, his mind and body were not. Again, he took a bus all the way across the continent, and this time, the distance was even greater, since Boston was so much further north. The days and nights were lost in agony before he reached his destination, and he arrived in Boston half-dead and in a sick and weary daze.

Mr. Campbell kindly met the bus at noon and took Gary immediately to lunch, which was both merciful and torturous. He craved rest and sleep more than food. But lunch was pleasant, and Gary kept himself under control.

Mr. Campbell was entertaining and expressed full confidence in Gary. He made some promises for the future that Gary did not entirely grasp at the moment, but he was grateful for the knowledge that all was not in vain. And now, if he could just find a place to lie down and sleep for twelve to sixteen hours, he would probably be as good as new, he felt. But he forced himself to sit and listen in a vague way to the voice that was not always clear.

He drifted almost into blacking out, as he was so tired and sleepy. But the words floated in and out of his consciousness as he sat, hopefully not swaying, across the white-clothed table from Mr. Campbell, who was saying many important things.

Rhode Island seemed to be the center of his topic, and Gary tried hard to listen as the food, quiet atmosphere, and lack of jarring by the endlessly turning bus wheels lulled him into a somnambulistic state. But through the fog drifting in his mind, a bit of information suddenly startled him wide awake. "Tonight" was the word that had shaken him, and he hoped he had not heard what he feared he had heard. "They were expecting you tonight," Mr. Campbell finished as he repeated part of what he had said.

"Tonight?"

"Yes. Tonight. I hope you're not too tired. They really are expecting you. Will you go?"

"Just so I don't have to take a bus," Gary answered hazily, practically in his sleep.

"Oh, of course not," Mr. Campbell agreed, laughing. He handed Gary the keys to a Fellowship car, a small Chevrolet, and began giving him directions for getting from Boston to Rhode Island. Gary fingered the keys. He had not driven a car for seven years.

It was early afternoon then, and it took him most of the rest of the day merely to get out of Boston, but at last, he was on his way to Rhode Island and headed for a new life—if he lived through this one.

His nerves were clanging and jangled when he finally arrived in Rhode Island, and he was too tired to do justice to a late supper. But he found himself suddenly before an audience; and to his surprise, words were coming from him that must have truly been inspired by God, because he had no idea of what he was saying. Then it was over, and he was in bed and asleep almost before he had flicked the light off in the little hotel room. He slept until the next afternoon, when he was awakened by a worried minister of the church where he had spoken.

Soon, he was off again on the next leg of his tour, and then another. Quickly, he learned to vary his message to keep himself from being bored. On and on he went to the myriad of small churches awaiting him on his New England circuit. Sometimes he even read excerpts from his one-man show, *The Weeping King,* which he now called *Great Moments in the Scriptures.* At other times, he simply shared his own testimony, and both of these variations seemed to engross his audience far more than a straight sermon. He was really surprised. He had actually become a sort of religious superstar to these people. They took a terrific interest, especially in his testimonials.

He found himself invited and welcomed at churches on the tour list that demanded him. It seemed that those on his tour had publicized his background as a former Hollywood denizen, which seemed to set him totally apart in the religious world. He was lionized and surprised that this should be. For his part, after he had been a witness a few times, he would rather forget about Hollywood and give his message of Christ.

But this was not allowed. The demand was for witnessing, and the subject was Hollywood, and he was not permitted to misunderstand this or to change his repertoire at will. They knew what they wanted, and they demanded it. The choice was no longer his.

Actually, Gary was more than surprised. He was, indeed, more nearly shocked. He was also a little wary of these people, because he had always heard that New England was a cold country in more ways than the weather. He was therefore amazed at the interest they evinced in his witnessing where it concerned Hollywood. Perhaps these people were more emotional than they seemed to be, he thought. He tried to encourage himself to believe that sooner or later, he would be accepted in real Christian fellowship rather than as a curio whom they felt entitled to probe.

To believe that Gary's leap from Hollywood to the grim, rigid righteousness of New England was a pleasure would be a grave mistake. It was grueling, and it was almost as disillusioning as Hollywood had finally been. If he had expected he was only going to exhort these New Englanders for Christ, he was soon disenchanted. The good evangelicals of New England, at least those to whom Gary spoke, were much more interested in Hollywood than any gospel messages.

His cinema exploits of which he had spoken were only such as he would part with, and were touched upon very lightly, but they seemed to be of far more interest to most of those good people than was the Lord's Word, he very quickly discovered. And then, one night on his tour, he found himself in Gardner, Massachusetts at the church of the warm and friendly Reverend Phil Wahl.

After delivery of a message he was proud of, with no demand for witnessing, Gary was introduced to those in the congregation, among whom were Lillian and Arlie Wiita, chicken farmers of Finnish descent, like himself. It was as if they had known each other all their lives. The all-embracing Christian kindness of this unpretentious couple endeared them to him at once. They were like family. He was delighted to find it had been arranged for him to spend the night with them.

He stayed nearly a year. Like "the man who came to dinner," he became a permanent guest. Far from the starting point of his tour now, he needed a place to stay, though he still had to travel. A brother of Arlie Wiita was also a guest. Eino was as cordial to Gary as his brother, Arlie, and it was hard to believe that both men were former alcoholics.

After years of drinking, suffering, climbing on the wagon, and falling off, Eino, the elder brother, had finally been converted to the Lord in the church and healed of his addiction. But his brother, Arlie, husband of Lillian and father of several children, was as much an alcoholic as Eino had been and had become a true derelict. He was drunk all the time and living in the gutters. He had become so in bondage to alcohol that his wife and children had left him. His wife, Lillian, whom everyone called Lil, had totally lost patience with him and given him up.

That had shaken him at the time, and he had later gone to his wife and on his knees sworn off booze forever. He had wept, and with tears in his eyes, promised her he would drink no more. But she had heard it all before and did not believe him. So he went back to drinking, taking that for an excuse. Eino was the only one who had still stood by him at that time. Having been converted and healed of his own addiction, Eino wanted badly to help his younger brother and knew it could be done only through the Lord.

Like many other alcoholics, Arlie was not at all eager to be helped. He seemed to prefer his misery. For a long time, Eino had tried to persuade Arlie to let the Lord help him, as Eino knew He could, but to no avail. Then one day, Eino had persuaded Arlie to promise to go with him to a service in a church that was holding its services in a storefront in Gardner, Massachusetts. This happened to be a Palm Sunday service, and Eino was very happy as he waited in front of the temporary church for Arlie.

Arlie showed up, but he was completely drunk. There went all of Eino's good intentions. He felt his heart would break. But his brother had shown up—albeit very drunk—so Eino decided they would still attend the services. He would ask God's forgiveness for his failure with his brother and pray that the light would someday come to Arlie.

Eino listened to the sermon and prayed while Arlie swayed on his bench seat beside him, breathing rancid fumes into the air. *Poor Arlie,* Eino said to himself. He would have to give him up. And his heart broke for Arlie's wife, Lil, and their children, as well as himself for losing a brother who would accept no help.

Eino became interested in the sermon, which was very good, and paid little attention to Arlie, only hoping he could sit up for a while longer without falling off the narrow backless bench. But imagine Eino's surprise, when he looked again at Arlie, he seemed to be following the sermon. How he could with such an alcohol-sodden brain, Eino didn't know, but it appeared that Arlie was listening. *Good,* Eino thought, *at least perhaps he is sobering up a little.* And then a miracle happened.

Somehow, during the invitation to come forward, Arlie heaved himself up and went forward on his own to confront the Lord. That was the turning point. Soon after that, Arlie was completely off alcohol, united with the Lord, and reunited with his family. And only a little later, he had become a dedicated and dynamic Christian worker, helping others.

Now when Gary met him, he was a fine family man and a good church member. Gary felt very fortunate to know both Eino and Arlie as well as Lil and their children. They were all fine people. And as Gary looked into the faces of the two men who still bore the ravages of earlier sin, he saw erasing, through the cleansing blood of Christ, this new triumph of salvation. They were new men—and fine men—and he thanked the Lord. He had found so much to talk about with Arlie that he had invited him to accompany him on the rest of the tour. Gary felt it was a blessing to have a native guiding him in that unfamiliar country.

Arlie showed the same constant enthusiasm for the work of the Lord that Gary did as an ordained minister, and he made a fine companion. Gary needed someone, and Arlie was the best. He bolstered Gary when the flesh was weak, causing him to object to the grueling routine of the church circuit. Gary had never known the circuit was so cruel. He was not amazed at those who dropped out from this merciless, grinding apprenticeship whose originators never made the tour.

Arlie would stand by Gary's side at the added ordeal of the coffee socials, which were mainly attended by gushing matrons who wanted to know as much as possible about the sins of Hollywood and cared about nothing else. Arlie would place a strong, steadying hand on Gary's arm to quiet him just as he was goaded into telling some of the clucking parishioners that there really were other things to think about. The quiet, truly Christian little town of Gardner seemed a beacon in the wilderness to him during this time.

Later, Gary would think about his irritation with the New Englanders and ask himself why he so objected to their affected and studied social manners. Was it because he had done the same thing at a certain time in his own life in fitting into Hollywood's stylized customs? At least, he ruthlessly scolded himself; these people were doing their gushing in church, while he had done his in nightclubs and parties in Hollywood, among the selfish and the sinful. And he had never given a thought to how offensive he might have been to others. So now, he tried to be more tolerant and understanding and Arlie helped him greatly.

He had not anticipated staying a year with these wonderful people, the Wiitas, but they had offered their kind invitation to use their home as his own and to make it his home base during the rest of the tour. He was delighted to do so. And with Arlie accompanying him on his tour, it was convenient, while Arlie also helped him to combat the loneliness of hotel and motel rooms and the constant solitary driving from place to place the tour required.

At the end of the itinerary, which consumed almost a year, Gary was surprised to find he was actually reluctant to leave, but there was no way to prolong the tour. Its purpose had been accomplished, and he was definitely a seasoned minister now. So he went home to Calumet, Michigan for a while to stay with his parents and see his sister for a long-overdue holiday, which he thoroughly enjoyed.

Chapter 15

Free at Last

The weather in Calumet, Michigan was cold—most rejuvenating—and he was home. Even though it was not clear to Gary what the Lord wanted him to do next, he was quite happy to be spending the time with his family. Then a letter came from Pastor Phil Wahl. He told Gary he was planning to return to college to get his teaching certificate and that an interim pastor would be needed in Gardner, Massachusetts at his Grace Evangelical Free Church. He asked if Gary would be interested in this position, which would be for six months.

Gary was delighted. Nothing could have been more pleasing to him. He saw it clearly as the Lord's answer to his prayer for a position. This was plainly the Lord's work. He was being prepared for bigger things. First, he had asked to be delivered from Hollywood and its subtle eroding effects, and he had been sent a tour—a rigorous time of testing—and now an interim pulpit. Thus, he was being prepared by his Lord to become a minister of worth. And this offer also included the pastor's moonlight position of night clerk at the local hotel, a small but steady income to supplement the pastor's small pay. It was perfect.

He gladly accepted this fortunate package and set off joyfully to see his friends in New England again. The Wittas were delighted, and Gary felt he was being well taken care of by his Maker. At once, Gary found the Grace Evangelical Free Church to his liking, and he felt that God was giving him sufficient guidance to lead his parish as well as he could with a clear mind and a firm purpose.

Only occasionally now as he went about his pastoral duties in those following months did he remember the man without hope on Hope Street. That man seemed now distant and but vaguely recalled. He had been a different man then and had no connection with this man he was today, having chosen a higher road to travel. But toward the end of the six-month interim, which seemed very short, he had an inner experience that drew him back in memory to that very different man he had left behind him there in Hollywood. This was a visit to the grave of the great evangelist Dwight L. Moody.

He went with the Wiitas one day on a pilgrimage to Northfield, Massachusetts, not far from Gardner. For Gary, it was a strong echo of his experience at the crypt of Rudolph Valentino. As he stood by the grave of Moody, he saw in his mind's eye another dead man—the departed Garrison Gray of filmdom. It was gone, that dream—never to return. It had been only a dream, and he was glad to be awake and know that it had no reality.

The Gary who had been Garrison Gray of movieland no longer existed. At last, he was free. His dream was over, and he could live his real life. Perhaps the ghost of that man was still there, somewhere inside him, but he had chosen who he wished to be. He had gone down into the valley of decision; he had made his choice. He had suffered the fiery furnace, and the dross was burned away.

He was the man he wanted to be, and he was humbled there on that little hillside graveyard as he thought of a life so perfectly lived as Moody's had been. Moody had also chosen. And the grave of his faithful wife was there beside his in the pastoral surroundings they had loved so well.

As he stood beside the grave of that good man, Gary felt a precious peace come to him that he would never lose. How different this was from the inspiration he had received at the grave of Valentino. That inspiration had forced to gouge, kick, fight, pit his lowest wits against the most base wits of others, scrabble, grasp, win at any cost, and never rest. How degrading it had all been. But when the inspiration is such a quiet humble man as Dwight L. Moody, then one need only be grateful, make oneself available to one's Maker, and serve Him in that same humble spirit.

As Gary thought of these things in the car on the way back with the Wiitas, he suddenly felt his cares falling away. He was no longer troubled by the fact that within another month, he must be uprooted, his interim position ended, and he had nowhere to go. He somehow felt a spiritual uplifting as they left the graveside and was actually looking forward to some sort of mission. Without the slightest reason, he felt that one was about to rest upon his shoulders. This seemed strange to him, since he knew quite well there was no possibility at the moment of any mission at all other than the temporary one he held and would soon relinquish.

He must face reality, he cautioned himself. He was still being carried away with his feelings about the great man, Moody. The ringing in his head of the words he had not uttered but thought at the gravesite—*I am ready; oh, Lord, I am ready*—seemed foolish and impatient. He tried to quiet his thoughts on the way back to Gardner. But he felt fidgety, and the words came louder inside his head. *I am ready. I am ready.*

He had been ready for a long time, he assured his mind as they entered Gardner and drove through the town. Whatever the Lord wanted would be, not his own declaring, *I am ready. So be quiet,* he told himself. *The Lord will tell me when. But wouldn't it be wonderful, he thought, if the Lord was ready, too, and my next mission was a church of my own?* He could almost envision something vaguely in his mind.

Oh, but that's ridiculous, he rebuked himself, with the chimerical picture fading further away. *It's possible, so pay attention. People are talking to you.*

"What did you say?" he asked Arlie.

"Mission Street. On Mission Street ..."

What a coincidence—just when I was thinking of a mission. Well, things like that happen, he told himself, paying little attention.

"And it's down here. On a dead-end street," Arlie said.

"What is?"

"Remember, I told you. It's closed now." Arlie was chattering at his side in the car as they drove down the narrow street called Mission. And then he saw it, standing at the far end of the street—a picturesque little white church.

A light, fluttery chill ran up Gary's spine. It was simply sitting there—empty, closed, shuttered—waiting. And it had been there all the time. It was almost too much. Gary felt a flush of goose bumps flow over him. He thought he must be dreaming, but he knew he wasn't. It was there waiting for him.

"Why is it closed?" he almost whispered to Arlie with awe as they left the car and stood, looking.

"Well," Arlie said briskly, "this little church has been here a long time. It was established before the turn of the century, folks say. It was built by Finnish evangelicals who wanted a church of their own to worship in their own way, so they build this special little church."

Gary gazed at the small church that had seemed to materialize before his eyes after he had prayed for just such a church for himself, never suspecting that what he saw vaguely in his mind's eye was already in existence and only waiting for his discovery. *Was this possible?* He wondered, and he realized with an odd feeling of lightheadedness that it was. It was actually happening to him.

In his daydreams of his own church, he had seen this little church—small, white, sturdy, strong, simple. And here it stood, waiting for him; it had been here all the time. Suddenly, he could not feel the ground under his feet. Something strange was happening to him. He must awaken. He should pinch himself, he thought without humor, and then he smiled.

The architecture, he realized now, making himself be realistic, was natural for him to picture in his mind, because it was reminiscent of churches in Finland and of those that his own Finnish ancestors had built in and around Trimountain and Calumet, Michigan, where his people lived. Naturally, this is what he saw in his mind; because it was familiar to him, and he loved it—and here it was, waiting for him. His own Finnish people had put it here.

They stood beside the car—an old Chevrolet that Arlie had kept running for years beyond its natural life. The others got out, and all four stood beside it, gazing toward the little church at the end of Mission Street.

"But you see," Lillian was saying, "the younger generation began to speak English, and as they grew up, they dropped their native tongue, and people began to fall away, I suppose. So they just deserted this little church …"

"For me. Just for me," Gary was whispering softly in a strange, awed voice.

"Toward the end," Arlie explained, "it didn't even have a full-time minister, and services were held only once a month or less by the minister of the Elm Street Congregational Church, Dr. William Summer, near here. And then, by that time, the Finnish congregation was so small that services were held only in the various members' homes. And now, just look at it. Isn't it sad?" he mourned. "But it's too rundown. Nobody wants it," he appended wistfully, turning away with the other.

"I do." In Gary's mind's eye, the old building was as beautiful as St. Paul's Cathedral in London.

"You do?" This was an animated chorus, and all three turned to stare at him.

"Yes. It's my church. I'm Finnish, and they left it here for me."

"I see it. It's beautiful. I've seen churches like this before. I love it."

"You do?"

"Yes. I can see worship taking place in there."

"You can?"

"Yes, and I can see those tall, silent, sober Finns building this for a church of their own. They'd build it as well and as strong as they built their fishing boats for those dangerous northern waters of their homeland," Gary mused, gazing, fascinated.

"That's almost poetry," Lillian said, taking a timid step forward. "No wonder people like to listen to you." And then she took another step and added, "I wonder what it's like inside?"

"Oh, very dirty. Old. Just like any old church," Arlie said pragmatically, sensible as always.

"But why did you never show me this before?"

"Never thought of it," Arlie said, waving his arm aimlessly. "Just always been here."

"Why today?"

"I dunno. Just thought of it. Just remembered it."

"Let's look in it," Gary suggested, stepping forward. He pictured in his mind a worship service taking place with joyous people giving thanks with hymns to their merciful and glorious Creator. He heard the inspirational hymns that would bring the lost forth to the Lord, as it offered them a new chance to enter the fold of Jesus. How wonderful he felt, seeing himself in his mind's eye with arms upraised on that pulpit, with planks so old and weak he would probably fall through, he thought, smiling suddenly, coming back to the present.

Through windows so cracked and dirty that he could hardly peer through them, he saw in reality the dusty, empty sanctuary, and he saw the light. It was shining through the little church from several holes in the roof. But it was beautiful, he thought as a surge of excitement went through him. This sturdy old church was surely not irreparable. "Would it be available?" he asked.

"I dunno, but we can get the key from Reverend Summer. He must still have it," Arlie said. "He's retired and lives near here."

Reverend Summer gave them the key with his blessing, and they returned to the little building. Gary suddenly felt a wonderful sensation of possession as they came up again to the front door. He opened it himself, feeling privileged indeed.

"In his entire earthly ministry, our Lord never entered such a structure as this of His own in which to teach," Gary said, feeling a sense of awe as they entered. "He was obliged to preach on hillsides, in friends' homes, and in the hostile temples of Jerusalem. He never had the blessing I am now experiencing," he reminded himself and his companions.

No one answered. They were all staring silently around. And Gary knew somehow in his heart, feeling blessed, that he was about to become the undershepherd of his mission church on a street named Mission.

This was his church. Somehow, he would buy it, though he had no idea at the time how he could.

Old wooden chairs, covered with dust and warped by the rain coming in through the ceiling, had obviously been crafted by the same hands that had long ago built the church. And the pulpit stood proud and solid on the platform in front, covered with dust but looking as if it had been there forever, waiting to hold a Bible again.

Gary stood in the pulpit created so long ago and so solidly built and looked out over the congregation that was invisible to all but him. He bowed his head in a prayer of real supplication and asked that God would guide him in the resurrection of this ancient and patient church and make it his own.

He would do his best here to make it come alive again—to lead well those who came to God's door. He thanked his Maker for leading him to this little abandoned church on Mission Street—his church.

But the other three who were with him were practical and had already pragmatically begun to clean, also knowing that this was his church. They could see it and feel it. The work that lay ahead, formidable as it would be in the little sanctuary that had stood alone for so long, was not too much for them. Gary soon set about with them to make this church his own—a gift he felt he had received from the loving hand of Jesus.

Chapter 16

The Little Church

It was a gift of God. There was work to be done. Besides the cleaning, shared by all four, there was a need to find members to fill the little church once it was cleaned and repaired. And the repairs were no small matter—especially the roof. But they set to work with a will to find the help they needed to make the little abandoned church a place of worship once again.

They contacted the past members of the Mission Street Church, as it had simply been called, and learned that some had still been praying that the church would someday reopen. These good Finnish people were willing and eager volunteers. In Finland, helping a neighbor raise a barn or carry a boat to shore was nothing special, and so it was with the church. Many came forward to help as they went among the parishioners, who gained others who had never attended but would love to if the church was made available for their own special worship.

There were many to help, and it came about that they did not actually need to ask for anything. The eager parishioners, of which the many were no more than a dozen or so, found, gave, and contributed all that was needed to rebuild the little church. And so, like when

Zerubbabel and Joshua were commissioned to rebuild the temple, it was done.

One of the most faithful of the former congregation was Miss Anna Hurnanen, a true saint whose long service as a visiting nurse in the community had comforted many. She had been in daily prayer for the little church she loved to be reopened. And while she could no longer function as a nurse because of advanced emphysema, she still functioned as a saint. A tiny woman of immense vitality and soul, her spirit was rejuvenating to all.

The work to repair the little church was hard and long, and the money to hire much skilled labor was short, but Gary helped by his interim pastoring, nearing its end, and his night work at the hotel desk, which continued. He also contributed what he could do in the manual work of the renovating project. Slowly, the church began to look active and even joyful. The soap and water work was endless, but the fresh paint made it shine.

Added to this were just a few spirit-filled believers. They felt this was another temple of Jerusalem, and Gary was humbled with thankfulness. He could see the church as it should be—ringing with joyful song, worshippers filling the seats. Their spirits overflowing with the love of the Lord, they would be coming in numbers to worship in the little church—the very first church of his own. Gary was happy and rejoicing, thanking the Lord for His bounty and goodness.

It was not a fancy place, of course. It was humble, small, and very old. The town of Gardner, having transferred even the most faithful of the little church's former members to its large, airy, clean, and beautiful Grace Evangelical Free Church, was loath to relinquish any of its congregation now. The members of that congregation were themselves very skeptical of his new little church. Why should anyone want to sit in a drafty, dark, and close little church, smelling of age and bare of comfort? Why should one sit on those ancient, hard wooden chairs when they could be seated in comfortable, familiar, and beautiful surroundings in the big church, as they were accustomed by now to doing?

So only the hardiest of the former members were interested in renewing the little church or becoming a member of such an outrageous upstart of a church as this. It was a bag penny. It had been abandoned once, even before it had become as rundown as it now was, and the town of Gardner was not inclined to give it much chance for revival. They were not going to disturb their dear Pastor Wahl, who had now returned to his church, by attending even one service in this appalling little church that should, in their opinion, have been left to rest in peace. But to Gary, still a night clerk, and the few disciples who worked so hard with him, it was a beautiful little church—humble though it was—and they loved every lowly aspect of it.

Gary had planned a first service that would stir the congregation and make them realize that souls could be saved in humble churches as well as in large, beautiful, and powerful churches. His purpose in life was the saving of souls and inspiring as many people as he could to give their lives to Christ. He felt this work could be done as well in a small, shabby church as in a fine, large, handsome one. He was setting out to prove it with the help of those who loved the little church as he did, and his faith was unconstrained.

The work required to refurbish and renovate that small building was prodigious. It seemed as impossible as their task must have seemed to Zerubbabel and Joshua when they were commissioned to rebuild the fallen temple. But they had done it, and Gary and his faithful followers, though few, had done this monumental chore. At last, it was ready.

A month's rent was paid on an electric organ, and they had pooled what was left of their meager resources and personal funds for newspaper ads announcing the reopening of the Mission Street Congregational Church. To Gary, this had a glorious sound.

It was a gala day, and there was joy in Gary's heart when he awoke on October 7, 1962, a little over a year after he had left Hollywood. This was the Sunday that would mark the opening of his first very own church. The date had been determined by the completion of their renovating work. But later, this date was found by the study of the annuals of the original congregation of the nineteenth century when the church was built to have been the exact date of the first service in 1894, just sixty-eight years before. To Gary, this coincidental date was God's way of saying, "Job well done."

The town of Gardner was not receptive, and their rejection of the new church was soon realized to be for more reasons than those due to their choice of a place of worship. Several businesspeople around town had been eyeing that little well-built structure for other purposes. They had seen it as having distinct possibilities for their enterprises, and only Reverend Summer, the keeper of the key, had kept the building off the market for anything but a church. His sentiment was adamant, but he had been almost ready to accede to their demands because of pressure when Gary had called for the key. Gary's plans for a church to be reestablished had made the pastor turn the key over to him with rejoicing and good will.

A local funeral director had recently been considering buying the building to use as a storage room for coffins. Another businessman had thought a tavern would be a novel thing to turn a church building into, and an oil company had been dickering for some time about buying it. They planned to tear the building down and put up a gas station. Now these businesspeople were all very upset to see the place being cleaned and renovated, and they and their spouses, families, friends, and relatives were no small part of a town as tiny as Gardner.

So with such opposition as was present, Gary should not have expected a large congregation for his opening, or even later. There were many reasons why another church, and especially that church, was not exactly welcome in that particular little town in Massachusetts. Gary knew this, but his faith was such that since the miracle of finding a dream church of his own had happened, he felt God would bring about other miracles as well. He had great faith.

His faith was rewarded. On that first opening Sunday, he had a congregation. True, it was not large, but he was grateful for not having to speak in an empty church. Emotion almost overcame him as he looked out over the seemingly beautiful newly renovated interior with tears gathering in his eyes. Stepping proudly up to the pulpit that had been built long ago to be strong and lasting, he was prepared with something close to a bursting heart to address his very first own congregation in his very first own church.

It was a day of crowning glory for him. He had prepared and labored hard for this, and now he was ready to deliver an opening message such as no pastor in any of the finest churches could emulate. No congregation anywhere, hearing this message from his heart, would ever be able to forget it. He was beginning a new era in devotion and worship of our Lord Jesus Christ, and all of his dreams were coming true.

He had practiced his written sermon until it was letter perfect. It rang with fervent love of his Maker and with enough inspiration to lead all lingering souls to the front at the invitation. When it ended, he raised his arms prayerfully in thankfulness to Christ for the fulfillment of his most fervent supplications and prayed for a bountiful benediction upon his congregation. They numbered six.

His powerful pulpit voice, in perfect diction, rang out hollowly over the empty chairs. The church could hold at least 150 souls. It contained (including himself) seven. Six were huddled together in the center and far to the front, and the whole high-raftered, dark, and empty church yawned around them as if to swallow them. They looked so small. There were Arlie and Lil, Mrs. Valija Balins, Mrs. Elsie Chipman, Mr. Ornie Herk, and Mrs. Eva Couture. And to them, Gary gave his best.

Never in all his nightmares had he dreamed of hearing his voice ring out so hollowly in such an empty church, exhorting the lost souls to come home, bringing the sweet words of Christ's forgiveness to souls already long saved. There was not a lost soul in that congregation to come forward. If Gary could ever question, if he could ever doubt, if he could ever stray from his chosen path, leave his calling, and wander the earth, he would have gone that week.

Only his tremendous and unshakable faith in his Lord could have kept him steady during those days of torture and doubt. His feeling of failure at times made him ill, and only the trusting, loving faces of his small, select congregation made him able to work on another sermon for the next Sunday that would be more suitable for the tiny, familiar group of faithful followers.

But the next Sunday, there were eight in the congregation, including Eino, who had been ill. And this time Gary was better prepared. His lesson was brief and simple, and he knew by their rapt attention that he pleased his loyal little knot of listeners. The next Sunday, there were ten. And they were all a closely knit group. They were all old friends to each other, and they loved their pastor beyond caring about anything but hearing his words to guide them on their path through life.

The group stayed small for a while, and they bolstered each other in keeping the Lord's commandments. All had a distinct sense of being like those original little churches in those first centuries after Christ. They regarded the town's skepticism as the first Christians must have regarded the derision around them in Jerusalem from the Romans and Jews alike of that time. Christ and His doctrine had not been accepted by many in those days, so through this modern town's cynicism, expecting and intending the eminent demise of this little upstart church, its small congregation clung together, faithfully gathering more as time went by, slowly and steadily increasing in numbers.

And while the town waited for the inevitable failure of the little church, which was avidly anticipated, its small congregation was resting on Romans 8:28: "And we know that in all things God works for the good of those who love him, who have been called according to His purpose."

Faith, Gary had learned, consisted quite simply of believing what one cannot see to be possible and knowing that God works miracles whenever He pleases to do so. Gary was asking for a miracle and believing it would happen. He was going ahead on that assumption, feeling in his prayers no rebuke or caution but sensing an instinct to forge ahead, believing that God was guiding him.

After the first shock of knowing that the little church was not going to bloom quickly, he resigned himself cheerfully to the circumstances. He found the situation good. He no longer had aspiration of becoming a big church, because he could see the advantages of a small church. The seven original members, including himself, did not picture long lines of people filing in to hear the services here or large groups coming to Christ before their humble pulpit. They were not concerned with this; they were concerned only with pleasing God and themselves and working to make their lives acceptable to Him—finding peace and happiness in this life and heaven in the next by so doing.

They knew that for this, they did not need a large congregation, and that their efforts did not have to include a public relations program, an elaborate system of funding, or copious donations, as did large churches. They were happy in their small sanctuary that grew more and more familiar, and the yawning spaces around them did not make them feel so small anymore. They almost seemed to fill the church. They were a wonderful, close-communicating, small congregation that enlarged over the years—years that passed quickly.

Four years later, in 1966, another church that had also served the immigrants from Finland lost its pastor. The Reverend Eino Hamalainen had served long and well in Maynard's small town some forty miles from Gardner. He had built a strong, if conservative, church. Its name had meaning for Gary—the Mission Evangelical Congregational Church.

"Mission" had almost become Gary's middle name. A pulpit committee had been formed before the pastor died, and Gary had learned that his name had come up as a possible interim pastor. He had also heard that one person had said in one of their meetings, "Reverend Heikkila will never leave that little church of his in Gardner; it's his baby." But another person replied, "Well, he can have twins!"

Miss Lilidh Pekkala, a long-time member of the Mission Evangelical Congregational Church in Maynard, was not so easily persuaded. The good sister had her own ideas of what constituted a truly spiritual pastor, and they did not include a Hollywood background. She was immovable. She had seen the steps Gary had taken in his own parish to generate higher interest in church services, and she thoroughly disapproved.

She had not liked his changing the usual order of the service, rearranging the altar area, and she thoroughly disliked the creating of dramatic effects with special lighting. Also, she objected strongly to his occasionally wearing clerical robes and collar. The good and saintly woman could not possibly condone that. She called Gary an "ostentatious young man" and was certain no one to take the place of the blessed Reverend Hamalainen. She had a wonderful rapport with him and was very sincere in her prayers for a suitable replacement, but this Reverend Gary Heikkila, she declared, was a little more than she could take.

Nevertheless, she did confess to some that his methods did have a certain effect and that people were indeed being jarred out of their mundane complacency. But she would have no part of it. It was not what she had come to believe was required or wanted of a religious leader. It was not for her, she declared, or her church.

At a crucial point, the Lord had stepped in. She had a marvelous dream one night. She saw the former pastor in her dream, and she was shocked, because he was supposed to be with the Lord. Then she saw herself in the balcony of the church, looking down as the Reverend Hamalainen walked up the center aisle to the altar. And there, at the altar, she saw Reverend Heikkila, kneeling devoutly in prayer. In her dream, her dear pastor had walked up to him, placed his hand on Reverend Heikkila's shoulder. Then he looked up directly at her and smiled. She awakened knowing she would never forget so realistic a dream. No one needed to explain this dream to her. When morning came, she called Mrs. Hamalainen, who reported that she, too, had had the sensation of her dear departed husband's presence during the night.

It was too much. Knowing the Scripture concerning the placing of the mantle of Elijah on Elisha, Miss Lilidh Pekkala changed her position entirely and declared that she thought Reverend Heikkila must surely be God's choice as the Reverend Hamalainen's successor. She also consulted Reverend Keijo I. Aho, who had been coming in the interim to conduct monthly services in the Finnish language, and told him she felt at peace about this issue at last. Eventually, she became Gary's most avid supporter. She was tireless and extremely helpful in his ministry.

Gary was eager to have the Maynard pulpit, even on the interim basis, for it would allow him to leave the tedious night job he had held for four years at the hotel, since having two churches would be enough to support him in at least a possible style of living. The interim was brief. A few months later, he was installed as the church's fulltime pastor by the Eastern Finnish Evangelical Congregational Mission Conference of America. His twins began to prosper.

He now conducted services in both churches each Sunday morning. He did this by conducting an early service at 9:00 a.m. in Maynard, where he now lived in the rectory of that church. Then, driving his old car, subsequently replaced several times by other old cars when refusing to run while held together by baling wire and a devout pastor's prayers, he drove the forty miles to Gardner. There, he at least tried to begin the services at 11:00 a.m. Then he returned to Maynard until evening services demanded another hectic run.

To say he was busy would be an understatement, but he was extremely happy and used his tremendous physical strength to good advantage, serving the Lord well and vigorously. Neither church was allowed to suffer, nor his faithful service to both stand as a monument to his faith, strength, and stamina throughout these many years.

By the end of the first decade, the little church in Gardner had begun to be filled to its capacity of about 150 souls. It was voiced that a larger building should be built, since a new building would have more capacity and also be profitable. But Gary, still working intimately with his original group of six, saw things in a different way. They did not need to build a new building; they loved the old one. It had served them well and would for many years to come. It was true they had not made any profitable investments with the church's resources, but they did find that God works in a wondrous way.

One day, when the church attendance was at its full capacity, one of his members came to Gary and proposed a wonderful thing. It was suggested that they reach out by radio to those who could to come to their little church. Gary and his group of original followers were delighted with the idea. It seemed the perfect solution. But when they first tried to get their services on the local radio, they were told, "Sorry, we're over-programmed religiously." However, in time, with the Lord guiding them, this attitude yielded to prayer.

After a while, the question came, "How much air time do you need?" The poorbox of the little church had never received a gratuity from a millionaire, so they came up with a very simple radio production. It has never changed. Gary preached the gospel, and his congregation said they loved people into the kingdom. Gary's message did not vary much from week to week. It was "God loves you," and that was sum total of it. He preached Revelations 3:20: "Here I am! I stand at the door and knock."

Soon after they began broadcasting, however, their little church was reaching out with its message of faith and devotion to not only the 150 members who came to the church, but to a potential radio audience of some fifty thousand souls.

Gary had long realized he was not in a particularly godly surrounding in New England, which has never been a comfortable setting for evangelicals, but he persevered. The liberal churches flourishing in this area were originally begun by angry loyalists who settled there, and Unitarianism was also firmly planted. The slight comforts offered by social religion had long taken precedence in the area over the harder methods of salvation, but Gary's evangelical stand for the gospel has still had its effects. And while its nucleus of founders would not consider altering the original structure of the little church on Mission Street for expansion, the Lord had made a way for them to expand.

Chapter 17

More Acting

Beginning in 1956, with two churches to attend and a radio audience, it would seem that Gary was as busy as one man could be, but God works in a mysterious way to perform His wonders. Gary found that a dream he had given up was not to be realized. He became a movie actor after all, and nothing was further from his mind at the time.

It was impossible to work in films in Hollywood without a membership in the Screen Actors Guild, but the Guild also assisted producers in contracting actors on location. Should a film or even a part of it be shot on location away from Hollywood, the Guild contacted local people who were registered in the Screen Actors Guild (SAG) for actors to play the smaller roles while the company was in town. It saved them transporting all the minor parts actors and actresses to the various locations.

Gary still maintained his membership in SAG without thinking about it or expecting anything from it and had really forgotten about it. It was the last vestige of his Hollywood days, and he had thought all ties with Hollywood were broken. But Hollywood was evidently not to be dropped so easily.

It happened that a picture titled The Cardinal was being shot in a part of Boston, and they needed a tall young man who could play the part of a Roman Catholic priest. Since Gary was near there, in Gardner, and was known to be an actor, it was natural for them to call on him. For one flashing moment before he consented to take the part, he wondered if he should tell them he was a Protestant minister and could not take the part of a Catholic priest, but this impulse had been quickly overcome, and he consented. He signed up for an audition and practiced looking extremely devout; he felt there could be no deception in that.

When a movie is ready for viewing, it looks as if it were shot in sequence with one scene following another, but nothing could be further from the truth. Each scene is filmed in many tedious and torturous sessions. Some brief scenes that last for only a few moments are repeated and repeated until the cast and director are ready to scream with irritation and tiredness. Lines are changed, added, or subtracted from the actor's script without a word of warning or seeming reason.

The High Potentate of movieland is the director, and he may change his mind at any moment or even at the last minute. He may scrap a whole film that has been laboriously made, changing it entirely. Or he may arbitrarily switch roles already learned by heart and expect a new role to be memorized almost at once. He has no limits but his own.

The set always looks like a madhouse, and it is incredible that anyone knows his individual job or can do it. It is a pure miracle that no one is electrocuted by wires tangled insanely, has a nervous breakdown on the spot, or just simply runs away in despair. Some do that every day, of course, which adds length to the time of production and would surely be handled better by more rational people, but those who attain the position of power do not do so by their sanity but by their wits and brilliance in a particular area, which seems to preclude common sense, order, or normalcy entirely. To Gary the producer was normal, though, and the audition went well. He was hired for the part.

The director of this picture was the renowned Otto Preminger, and Gary's part was an important one that left him, after several other priests were tried out, in a scene with the two celebrated actors in the picture, Tom Tryon and John Huston.

Now, however, Gary's screen name was not used, and his real name was, and it was a thrill to see his own name appear right under Tom Tryon and John Huston and right above those of Peter McLean and Dino Deluca. These names were followed by Carol Lynley, John Saxon, Dorothy Gish, Maggie McNamara, and Jill Hayworth. Gary had really made it. He was right up there at the top with the stars.

The cast sheet was the important thing for him, however, and it was exciting to read:

Gary Heikkila	
CHARACTER	YOUNG PRIEST
6:45 a.m.	MAKE UP
7:30 a.m.	WARDROBE
8:00 a.m.	LV HOTEL
8:30 a.m.	SET CALL

There was no car, however, for Gary, as there was for those who had special cars: "Car for Miss Gish, car for Miss McNamara, Mr. Preminger's car" and so forth for the stars, but he was included in "one for the cast."

Gary was transported back to Hollywood by that familiar cast sheet. He hadn't slept a wink that night and was ready and eager to go in the morning. He had his makeup on and his costume in perfect order and was ready to "LV HOTEL at 8:00 a.m." even though he was actually leaving from the temporary studio headquarters with his heart pounding from excitement. But he hadn't forgotten to take time to thank God for this wonderful belated gift that he appreciated with all his heart. It was a wish come true, and he gave no thought to its long delay.

He was horribly nervous, however, when he was about to step in front of that big camera. He was afraid he'd slip, stumble, fall down, or even lose his breakfast. It flashed across his mind that Valentino would not have felt like this—or would he? Perhaps everyone was nervous.

Certainly, all were on edge; he was aware of that. Yet to his great pleasure, he went through his scenes as smoothly as he had rehearsed them.

Mr. Preminger was not to be impressed by anyone's perfection. He made them all do the scenes over and over again. It was *wait, wait, wait; repeat and repeat;* and *wait again.* The lights were hot, and the people were tired, even in the early hours because of the tension. It went on and on until finally, the director was satisfied; they then went on to repeat the same tedious procedure in future scenes.

When Gary considered this and realized that all actors did this all day long, every acting day, he began to reconsider the glamour of his dormant dream. Maybe he was the lucky one after all. Maybe he should thank God for what he had missed. No one enjoyed it, certainly. At least he enjoyed his work for the Lord, and he knew he wouldn't have enjoyed acting for very long.

Then at last, when he and the rest of the cast heard the beautiful words, "Cut it and print it," meaning the scene was done correctly; he was intensely relieved along with the rest of them. Unless some unforeseen changes were made, the scenes were over and would be run in the movie when it appeared. He, the Reverend Gary Heikkila of Gardner, Massachusetts, would be on the silver screen forever.

That moment of inner triumph was rudely interrupted by the stagehands striking the set. *Wham!*—and it was gone. It was hard to believe it had all happened and was now over. *That was acting?* He asked himself. He knew suddenly he was lucky to have escaped Hollywood.

Gary determined he would go home and thank God. He'd say to God, "You knew best, after all. I couldn't possibly have done that all day long, day after day. It's inhuman!" He remembered the Guild's instructions: "As a professional actor, you are expected to report to work on time with lines memorized."

Dear God, he thought now, *what a task they put before one. What magic fascination could make one continue with such a profession when all you ask is that we appear as we are? You don't require us to memorize our doctrine or messages that you put into our minds as we study your good book. You don't require that we play something we are not. You are no respecter of persons, and you don't care who rides in what car. You don't make us repeat, through some ridiculous whim, what we have already done perfectly. You don't construct a set for us and then tear it down before our eyes and leave us feeling empty and used up. The sets you construct are magnificent, lasting, and permanent, and they fill our hearts with joy. And beyond that is your promise that you have built a set for us in eternity. Why would I want the tinsel of Hollywood? Clearly that fiery furnace has refined my spirit. I see it all now in a different light.*

"Father," Gary prayed when he was again back home and locked in his routine of serving two churches, which was surely not an easy life, "I don't believe anything happens by accident in your creation. I know you have saved me from what I would have eventually come to hate. You have offered me this that I love, and I cannot thank you enough for giving me the church instead of a career in Hollywood. After that, Gary felt a new contentment enter his heart.

When he finally went to the movie theater to see The Cardinal, it was a unique moment. He could hardly recognize himself up there on the screen, larger than life. Then afterward, a humorous incident happened, and while Gary would not spoil the moment, he was sorely tempted when a lady gushed on about him carrying his "sister" (Carol Lynley) into the hospital so beautifully that she had simply broken down and cried. It had not been he but Tom Tryon who had done that. But he had not the heart to cause an anticlimax to her moment.

Not long after the picture was out, Gary got his second chance to be discovered, though he desperately hoped by now that he would not be. But he did not want to turn the role down and felt that since this was only a bit part of the film *Tell Me You Love Me, Junie Moon,* a fine love story about handicapped people, he took the part. Otto Preminger had explained simply, "We need a minister," so there seemed no reason why he should hesitate. He thoroughly enjoyed working in that movie, even though it had turned out to be every bit as hard work, concerning the matter of retakes, as *The Cardinal* had been.

They shot Gary's simple scene as minister twenty-eight times. The scene was in a cemetery and a familiar one to Gary. His role was as a minister, officiating at a funeral scene shot in the old Manchester Cemetery near Boston. Gary had conducted funerals there, and he did not have to memorize anything. The many retakes had nothing to do with him, but he had to go through them and endure them nevertheless.

There were various things that kept happening to ruin the scene, and while many were minor and soon remedied by reshooting the scene, which was repeated time after time, there was one incident that was more trivial and caused several retakes to be made as a consequence. A dog was in the scene, and while Gary was routinely reciting the same old burial service over once more, the dog grew exceedingly restive and abruptly bit the actor nearest him, who happened to be James Coco.

This caused a stir and also caused the next few takes to be unusable. It later occurred to Gary, who was going over the scene again and again until he almost fell into a drone, because he was so familiar with his part and so tired, that the one whom the vexed dog really should have bitten was the director. But the best part of the whole movie for Gary was working with Liza Minnelli. She was so professional, such a good sport, and so friendly and outgoing—off screen as well as on—that it was a delight to work with her. She introduced Gary to her dog, though understandably, Gary was a bit down on dogs at the time, having barely survived the retakes caused by another, but he was polite. Liza also posed with him for photos he would always cherish.

The making of that film was not Gary's only tribulation. After all those retakes, the time, the trouble, and the effort put into them, the whole episode was boiled down to one very short scene. And after most of the cutting room floor, he saw in the final showing that he had been left but a minuscule moment on the screen in which to say only one solitary word—"Amen." Of such crass brutalities is Hollywood composed.

It was devastating to compare this end result with the amount of work that one word had required of him. The thought of a single word having put him through the torture of dawn appearances, lights, cues, makeup, stance, intonation, and perfect enunciation of whole long paragraphs of the burial service, repeated over and over, only to have this solitary word survive, gave Gary deep thoughts on the subject of earthly justice.

There followed *The Thomas Crown Affair,* casting in another location, which broke his religious typecasting and allowed him to meet some exciting people whom he would always remember. During this picture, he met Steve McQueen and Faye Dunaway—a tiptop actress, in his estimation—and he liked them both. He found them very human and normal people and enjoyed knowing them and the others he met in the cast. Of course, in between these moving picture engagements, he attended to the ministry of his twins, and both were progressing satisfactorily.

His next filming opportunity brought him to know Patty Duke and Ted Bessit in a TV filming project titled *Two on a Bench* in which Gary played the interesting part of an FBI agent. The scenes were done on the Boston Common, which made a very accommodating movie setting.

He began to receive more TV appearances after that and appeared on TV in Washington, New York, and also back again in Michigan. He was on in one spot with Hal Holbrook of the wonderful Mark Twain program. Gary did not hesitate now to let his Hollywood friends know of his faith and his work. In fact, he often wore a clerical collar to show that he was proud of his calling and would never again hide the fact that he was a bona fide minister, making this plain even in TV and radio interviews.

In an NBC radio interview in New York City, he praised the Lord openly, making his faith perfectly clear to the audience as well as the interviewer, which gained much approval from the audience. He now had more TV and radio interviews offered than he could accommodate and had to turn some down for lack of time. He still made many TV appearances and felt that his popularity was due mostly to the unique combination of his different pursuits. He did not hesitate to make it known, however, that being a minister was his vocation, and he would never cease to praise the Lord and make his faith known to all.

He was aware that he was regarded by some people in the media as a sort of Holy Roller and was sometimes invited to shows for the attention his two noticeably incongruous careers drew. They seemed to most people to be about as far apart as the poles, and it amazed some that a person could comfortably employ themselves in both pursuits at once. Yet this was the mystery of Gary—that he could do both very well and keep them separate and apart while remaining integrated in his knowledge and sincerity in dealing with both. It did not annoy him that some thought of him as an ambitious actor and others knew him as a dedicated minister. He was both, with no apologies.

The time came when the pressures of his church life left him little time for an avocation, and he gave up what was least essential to him. He felt, however, that he had perhaps given up too soon when he began turning down all movie parts and was to always feel some regret in having turned down a part in *Love Story* that he was offered. But he was not flexible enough to grasp it, since he had decided by then to appear in no more pictures. He knew his true calling was with the Lord, which would give him his real satisfaction in life, while acting was a passing predilection that he indulged in only up to a certain point.

He was to later feel strongly that he had made an error in judgment in turning down the part in *Love Story* that he had relinquished reluctantly. This caused him to realize anew the ambivalence of human nature—an ambiguity with which most talented people are especially endowed. Again, he had been forced to come to the painful time of having to make a choice. He made it, feeling that at that point, his acting career had run its course. He no longer felt frustrated, as he had in Hollywood. Now he was ready to correlate his energies into one channel and concentrate on his main theme in life—religion and its various ramifications.

He gave up acting willingly and freely, because he had two churches to attend, and he realized there was no way he could accomplish anything by spreading himself too thinly. By digressing into the field of filmdom, he would have had to neglect his churches, which he could not bring himself to do. He had to give up something, he knew, and he came to realize that, of course, it had to be the pursuit that he had told himself was an avocation, not a vocation. So he turned again solely to his real calling—the ministry. But while he had given up his avocation willingly under the pressure of serving two churches, he was to find that human nature is not the amenable slave it is thought to be.

As noble as Gary felt his choice to be and as convinced as he was that he was choosing the right path and following God's will for his life, there was no escape from the dreadful scourge of depression that now settled down upon his soul. This subordinate talent he was finding, though he was not conscious of it, was not so easy to subdue.

Again, without warning, it had come—this terrible depression. In the midst of his desperate ambition to fill the void that dropping his secondary talent had created within him, and though he was still extremely busy, an inner battle began, of which he was not even aware and could not control.

He knew what having to make a choice would mean, because he had tried it before. Then, when he had at last felt he had conquered this willful side of his nature, he had been enticed back again by unexpected parts in movies being suddenly offered to him. This had happened because he still belonged to that subconsciously buried actors' guild, which had found him for pictures made on location. Suddenly, all his ambition and talent had come flooding back with the first part he played.

He had long told himself that acting was his secondary talent and desire. He had believed that ever since his painful experiences in Hollywood, where his efforts, intentions, dreams, and desperate wishes had all gone for naught. But suddenly, this secondary talent had seemed to bloom again and become strong. Once more, he had to submerge it and make a choice between two loves.

Again, he had to make up his mind that acting was the secondary talent of his character. When he could no longer indulge in both talents and was forced to choose, he must choose again to follow the ministry. He felt this would make him the most happy and fulfill God's will for him. But a conscious choice does not always coincide with a subconscious choice.

He was aware now that his acting talent was not his paramount talent for which the Lord intended him, though he was mightily tempted to make his first talent and give it its worldly satisfactions. In this mood, he chastised himself for having turned down the one movie part that could have done this. But through prayers and supplication, he came to know that while he loved acting, it was his secondary talent, and it was the one to give up. His first talent lay in the ministry and in service to Jesus, and this was the more pleasing to his Maker.

Yet now despondency had descended upon him without notice or warning, and he was helpless in the grip of a deep depression. Inner conflict and decision is a painful but necessary process, and all must suffer in its flames to some degree. He knew this, but why must it be? He implored this of Jesus in the midst of his pain.

Receiving no answer, he suffered. In the throes of subconscious indecision, he suffered the torment of hopeless despondency. In despair of ever measuring up to his own as yet unsublimated expectations, he sank deeper into a dark and hopeless depression.

Chapter 18

Despondent unto Death

At first Gary had felt he could fight his depression that had overcome him by keeping busy. But soon he found he was not to be distracted by work. The accompanying fears of an impending catastrophe instead distracted him from his work. Despondency invaded Gary's life with long hours of uncontrolled "blues."

The despondency of those prolonged morbid moods turned finally into self-destruction, since there seemed no end to the emotional pain, and the mental anguish he was suffering would not cease. In the weeks that followed, Gary thought much of destroying himself. Knowing suicide was sinful, he drove the thoughts deeper inside him, trying to dispel them by sheer force of will.

During this time, he came across a story of the life of Betty Hutton in a movie magazine. He felt a sudden kinship with her when he read that her depression had driven her to several suicide attempts, though she was a successful movie star at the time. In fact, she told that she had also just recently made seventeen consecutive hit records, had been paid more than ten million dollars for her film appearances, could command

$50,000 a week in Las Vegas, and had her own TV series. But she was so depressed that she had actually attempted suicide.

This appalled Gary. But as he read on, hoping to find comfort in her solution to her problem, he found that when Betty Hutton had finally decided to live and had come to the end of her emotional rope, she had called in a pastor and confessed to him, "I am lost." The pastor had known what to do for her. He had led her to her Maker.

This made Gary begin to think. The Lord had restored Betty Hutton and led her to a gracious and happy life, just as He had Gary's good friend, Arlie Wiita, years before. But what of Gary Heikkila? He was already saved, he thought bitterly, but was despondent unto death. What could he do?

Determined not to give in to his morbid suicidal impulses, Gary studied. He tried to learn to control himself but was not encouraged by the literature of the National Institute of Mental Health when he read that each year, in the US alone, four to eight million people suffered as he did. He now realized he was suffering from a quite common disability and that severe depression held the psychiatrist's deep respect. He also learned that some quarter of a million Americans each year are hospitalized with this malady and that the suicide rate among them is thirty-six times greater than it is among the rest of the population.

Naturally, Gary had turned to God constantly for help, as he always had, but in his state of mind, with his depression affecting even the way he thought, it became difficult for him to say even the most simple little prayer for himself—a thing he did constantly for others. But now, he felt so cut off from life, from himself, from others, and from God, that he was becoming convinced he could not cry out loud enough for God to hear him.

He did not realize that autism, created in the frame of mind that causes depression, was making him withdraw inside himself and be unable to accept anything or respond in any way. In autism, one becomes self-centered and feels bereft and deserted by God as well as man, and in this self-contained state, he or she sinks deeper and deeper into despondency. One descends into a state of exaggerated sadness and hopelessness that is accompanied by low initiative and reduced activity, even of the mind. And in this state of aloneness and self-centeredness, suicides are fostered, since one comes to feel that life had reached a dead-end.

It seemed to Gary that he was truly alone in the world, and this was furthered by the autistic impulse that made it seem important to him to keep his woes to himself. The vicissitudes of life seemed utterly crushing. Yet he sorely needed the human contact he was avoiding.

Depression, of course, is a common characteristic of the human condition and is cited many times in the Scriptures. Some of the most successful of the ancients succumbed to it. Job had a dreadful time. King David, the immensely successful and talented sovereign, fell under the terrible yoke of depression. So Gary with no ostensible reason was felled by depression, and he felt he could not even reach God with his prayers for relief.

Without realizing it, however much he struggled to find a reason, feeling that this would relieve his pain; he did the very things that caused more pain. He allowed himself to feel he was being punished for his sins. He forgot that Jesus taught there was no punishment, only forgiveness in His heart, and begged all mankind to be like Him—forgiving, even self-forgiving. Neither Jesus nor God ever punishes. We, in fear and anticipation of God's wrath, punish ourselves, and Jesus pleaded for us not to do this. He said to forgo vengeance even against ourselves. He said, quite simply, "Go, and sin no more." But Gary forgot. He forgot that Job was wrong when he thought God punished him, and so are we all.

Depression seems to come as a cloud over us, and we ask ourselves, "What have I done to deserve this feeling of futility, morbidity, lack of desire for anything, this awful dejection?" We feel we must have done something wrong to deserve this, and we dredge up what we can for a reason. But depression really comes from one source and one source only—a battle within our minds. And this is a battle we are not aware of with our conscious minds.

We are born a dichotomy. We all have two natures. Most of us have two talents. Some have more. But many have two main talents and two main personalities; even though they are not equal, both may be strong.

To be mature, we must have unity and be integral, whole, and complete. We are not easily integrated. We must sometimes struggle most of our lives for the integration of our two selves. Both wishing to influence us for fulfillment, they pull us two ways.

Gary had two personalities, as do most people, but he had two very talented personalities. Both were strong, and they clashed. One was very good, and the other would like to have been wayward and bold.

Fortunately, the stronger of his two personalities, despite its quietness, was the good one that was guided by his ego, not his id. This ego personality is controlled by the superego, wherein lies the conscience, which was highly developed in Gary. It knew the good, loved the good, and had felt the call to serve Jesus.

The other personality, as in all of us, is controlled mainly by the id. This side of us would like to enjoy the pleasures of the earth. This subconscious id will achieve its ends in any way possible. We feel it as a natural inclination toward pleasure, self-gratification, and satisfaction. It is not fond of obeying the superego or conscience. This id had tried to lead Gary astray in Hollywood during his determined attempt to become a star.

We all have a willful side. Let us not deny it. Gary was blessed with two sides to his nature as well as two talents. Once the willful side, influenced by his id, had its way in Hollywood, it would have known no bounds. Had it found its opportunities in Hollywood, it would have led Gary to be as soulless an actor as many before him have been and will be forever after. Of course, many fine actors are not soulless, but acting is their destiny, and unless they progress spiritually, it is as high as they can rise.

Gary had two almost equal sides. Both were talented, and since these two personalities must become integrated for human beings to develop emotionally to their highest potential, Gary was having a harder time to integrate than most—hence his repeated depressions.

He knew with his obedient side that he must be a minister—that he had been called and that this was his destiny. But to do so, the talented, extrovert, actor side had to be subdued and lose its force to the strength of the rigidly disciplined ministerial side. The two had to integrate for

Gary to have any success in life. But the two personalities were enemies. If one were to win, the other must be subordinated. Both had almost equal strength. So whenever one side of Gary aspired to become the dominant side, the other side fought for its existence.

Within Gary's subconscious mind, war was then declared, and a battle between the id and the ego had been fought all during Gary's sojourn in Hollywood. He could do nothing. It was fought out in his subconscious mind. But when he realized what success in acting in Hollywood would require of him, he had made a conscious choice. He had sided with his ego, which is controlled by the superego. He had decided he wanted to leave the acting field, and he turned first to the business world. Again, he felt the call and knew he must return to the ministry. But there was still an inner subconscious resistance from his id to this restricted life.

The willful side of the always-dual personality that exists in all human beings was very strong in Gary. It would not give up without a tremendous struggle. This conflict can cause a light or deep depression, depending upon its importance. We all, at one time or another in our lives, go through such depressions when these subconscious battles are fought within us.

Sometimes the only way the willful side, or id, which is not controlled by the superego, can win is by destruction. In this solution is suicide. If this suicidal impulse is weathered, the depression ends, because the battle has been won and is over. But it is not always won by the better side. In such cases, suicide may only be delayed.

Sometimes, when no strong conscious desire or goal is present, no decision is made, and the conflict goes on for a very long time—even a lifetime. Some people without a goal live lives of repeated depressions, and neither the id nor the ego wins. They continue to battle in long illness, dementia, or death.

Before his battle was ended, Gary's health began to break. He suffered greatly from stress. He prayed, but he found he was, even against his will, falling away and committing the one sin that even Jesus had little patience with—a lack of trust in God. He seemed to receive no help from his prayers and did not ask himself if he might have lost his faith. No, he told himself, no one can pray without faith. Jesus knew that and said so. But he was tired. He thought he was weary from the depression that had settled down upon him like a cloud, suffocating and weakening him. But he was really tired from the inner battle of which he was not even conscious. He took no part in it. He had already made his conscious decision. But the two sides of his nature participated in a subconscious tug of war.

He was not aware of the dual nature of man in the sense of his own subconscious battle; he only knew that he had asked for help, peace of mind, and inner peace and received it not. He was not aware that he must achieve this for himself by making a firm, conscious decision and sticking to it—putting it into action. Had he been aware of this, he could have consciously fought for the decision he had made by thinking of it consciously and thus reinforcing it and so have vastly shortened the war, as many have done and more have not.

But he was not aware, and he allowed himself to be a battleground for his inner forces, unperceiving and unconscious of what was happening, vacillating between two intense desires, not making a conscious choice, but letting his subconscious and his conscious minds battle freely, as we so often do to our prolonged pain. Were his prayers wasted? Was there no one up there? He asked this in desperation, wanting God to settle it, not himself.

It became a matter of life and death to reach God with his prayers. "Have mercy on me!" he cried. "Help me in my unbelief," he prayed, as Job had prayed for belief. He humbled himself as never before and prayed long and hard. Suddenly, he found that he was praying in faith. He was still not sure God would help him to get well, because he remained very sick and weak, but he had found his faith, so he had to believe that God had heard him. Mainly, he knew because his decision was reinforced to be content to be a minister.

He was still quite ill physically, but his depression was lifting. He was regaining a feeling of self-confidence. His inner choice had been made again. He felt that, and the feeling of well-being stayed with him. There was no longer any question in his head concerning his loyalty to the Holy Spirit or its power. He knew the Lord had told the disciples clearly that He would send them the "Comforter in their need. The baptism of the Spirit is imperative to living a Christian life and doing Christian work, and Gary had experienced that.

Gary, in his extremity, had given his life over completely to God. He had done this by reaffirming his conscious desire in his prayers. And through desire and prayer, his two personalities became integrated into one integral, whole person—one personality. He was not being pulled two ways but was one complete personality, with no talent wasted or los, but both devoted to the purpose of spreading the Word of God.

Gary decided then to make the most of both his talents. He asked himself, "Cannot the talent of acting be as important—if used in imparting a clearer picture in the minds of listeners in a congregation by subtle actions which convey emotions of sincerity, faith, and devotion—as it is in conveying other emotions in a theater or upon a screen?" The answer came to him—yes. What better way than to strike a pose, assume a posture, and express feelings as one speaks of the Lord? Would that not be the way to impress those in a congregation of the sincerity and belief of the minister who was leading them in the worship of the Lord?

How different and ineffective, by comparison, is the impression given by words spoken in a passive voice—a sermon presented with an inert pose, showing no emotion or rapport. How futile such a delivery would be of even the most beautiful, moving, and passionate words ever written if there was no accompanying expression, action, or demonstration of emotion or feeling for the words spoken. There would be little to stir the imagination in any words without some acting ability in delivering them, Gary began to realize.

He knew he stirred emotion in others when he expressed it in his voice and actions. Subtle as a minister's actions would be, still, there is some emotion displayed and responded to by his congregation. He realized now that he needed this second talent to use for the work of the Lord.

Without thinking of this consciously but through his prayers, Gary did what needed to be done. He sublimated his acting ability in his service to Jesus. He incorporated it into his sermons and thereby satisfied it—and himself emotionally—by so doing. He did not reject this God-given talent or submerge it completely. No talent should be suppressed. It would have disturbed him emotionally had he tried to do this. Gary simply began to use it in a different way. He sublimated it, and in a subordinate position, he allowed it to still exist. By integrating, he succeeded in preventing inner conflict from threatening or thwarting his principal purpose in life.

Chapter 19

Salute to America

GARY HAD HIT ROCK BOTTOM. He knew God was his only refuge. He gave himself entirely to God—his gifts, his talents, his all. He felt no regrets. His happiness kept increasing. He felt he was getting a new grip on life. He felt he understood much more as he read the Bible through and through. When reading the saga of Job, he felt as Job felt when he had said stoutly, "Though He slay me, yet I will trust Him" (Job 13:15). He also felt for the first time that he really understood Romans 8:28: "And we know that in all things God works for the good of those who love him, who have been called according to His purpose."

Gary knew without any lingering doubts what he wanted of his life. He wanted to devote his life to Jesus. He wanted to be a minister, and he would utilize all his talents to that end. No longer was there a battle within him. He had almost died over that battle, but now it was ended, and he could live the life he wanted to live at peace within himself. He had become an integral human being—a whole person.

At this time, Gary felt an urge to see the old city of Jerusalem, where he had flown the day before. Gary stood looking down the Mount of Olives, and he felt elated. The sunlight shimmering on the buildings below gave the stones a golden glow. The wall surrounding the Old City of Jerusalem zigzagged across the hillside, and the ancient Golden Gate in the foreground thrilled him as he stared entranced at the view. It burst upon him suddenly, because he had seen nothing the night before when his plane had landed at dusk. He had entered the city of the prophets the previous evening in the darkness, and after viewing this beautiful morning scene now glowing from his hotel window, he wanted to stand on scared Mount Moriah, where the temple had been.

When at midmorning he was there, he gazed also with awe upon the unbelievably resplendent Mosque of Omar. This is a most important Muslim shrine, and inside is a large rock believed to mark the spot where Abraham prepared to sacrifice Isaac. It is the place from where Mohammed was said to have ridden to heaven astride his famous steed, El Burak. And all of Jewish tradition acknowledges it to be the foundation stone of the temple.

In the few days that Gary could spend in the wonderful, historic city of Jerusalem, he absorbed the entire atmosphere he could to take back with him into his own world, where almost two thousand years later, he was still spreading the words that Jesus had spoken here in this faraway part of the world. He was promising yet the promises Jesus had made to mankind then. In 1971, Gary was proud to be able to spread the words of our Savior, which were still as important, misunderstood, ignored, and futile, at times, as were those same wonderful words when actually spoken by our Lord in this very spot.

Gary reflected that Jesus had not given up because some did not listen. So why should he, as a lowly Christian leader with a following of two churches? Was he not obliged to teach his fellow men what Jesus had taught there in robes and sandals in those long, long years ago? If he and others like himself, Gary thought with an aching heart, did not fulfill the obligation God had given His only begotten Son, then who would then carry on the Word to the souls that Jesus had given His life to save? Yes, he must carry the message on. He must forward the message Jesus had brought them of many mansions in the heaven He had come from and returned to, as all who breathed the breath of life would always do in the endless cycle of God's creation.

If men like himself, Gary thought—dedicated men who were willing to devote their lives to carrying Jesus' message to the world—did not carry out their missions, then many souls would be lost. The world would not hear the wonderful message that Jesus had brought and told of in His time in that glorious city. So Gary felt honored. With the blessing of the Holy Bible to work with, he could be a part of that army of dedicated ministers of God who were spreading the words of Christ abroad in all the land. He rejoiced in the burden that had been placed upon his shoulders.

Gary returned from the land of Galilee refreshed, renewed, and ready to take up his tasks of keeping two churches functioning and spreading the words of the gospel to all who would listen—and many listened. In the little church in Gardner where there was no parish house in which to live, Gary gave Sunday morning services from 11:00 a.m. to noon. While this little church held only about 150 people and was filled to capacity each Sunday, it reached out to others via its radio broadcast. This 11:00 appointment with the broadcasting station monitoring was an arduous duty to a pastor who had to rush from giving an earlier service from 9:00–10:00 a.m. at the Mission Evangelical Congregational Church in Maynard.

The distance of some forty miles that Gary had to drive in no more than fifty minutes was a strain in a succession of old cars held together mainly by prayers. That his prayers were fervent and fruitful, no one can doubt, for from 1966, when he took over the Maynard church, to the year of 1983, he made this required trip in slowly increasingly better cars each Sunday of his life. Then he returned to Maynard after these services in Gardner, because the Maynard church had a parsonage in which he lived for many years. During the week, he made this trip yet again for midweek evening services. No one can say his life has been easy.

That his social life suffered, there can be no doubt, but his dedication to his twins was sincere and lasting. Some of his parishioners, however, felt sorry for the rigid way he had to live, and many of them adored him in a loving and understanding way. The Wiitas would have liked to take him to still live with them in Gardner, but he felt he could function better from the parsonage in Maynard.

Then, later in 1971, his Mission Evangelical Congregational Church in Maynard found itself without an organist with the Thanksgiving service swiftly coming up. This was very important to them, and Gary appealed to his secretary—the church clerk, Miss Lilidh Pekkala—to find an organist as soon as possible. Lilidh knew a wonderful woman living in Maynard, Marion Jones, who was the organist for another Congregational church but might like to make a change.

Gary called her immediately and asked her to play for their Thanksgiving service. He thought she seemed upset but was totally unprepared when she told him she appreciated his call but was sorry she could not play for that service, because he had called at an instant when her dear sister lay on the front porch, having only a few moments before seemed to have suffered a heart attack. Poor Marion had answered the phone automatically and was about to call a doctor, unable to believe her sister had really succumbed.

Shocked and horrified, Gary rushed to her home in time to help her and comfort her when the ambulance came. He learned that her sister, Mildred, whom everyone called Dolly, had suffered a sudden fatal heart attack and died instantly. Marion Jones could not express her thanks to Gary for helping her in her time of need. His call, she felt, had saved her from being alone in her most terrible grief, as he had been there within a very few minutes and helped her to call the doctor. She would never forget the comfort Gary could give her at this most grief-stricken time in her life and later. Dolly, Marion, and a brother, Ralph, lived together. Marion herself had never married, and now she was devastated at being alone in her deep sorrow.

Marion became the church organist, and at her death in 1973, she willed the house in which she lived to Gary. It was a fine old home, and at least he could leave the parsonage, which was then rented out for church income. He had a home of his own for the first time in his life.

In 1971, when Marion Jones had first become the organist for the church, Gary had given his annual Salute to America services for four years. An article written about it in the *Beacon* on November 15, 1971 by a Maynard reporter had this to say: "'America's youth are turning to Christ by the thousands,' says Rev. Gary Heikkila, who despite all signs to the contrary, finds good reason to be optimistic," and then continued, "The minister, Rev. Heikkila, pastor of the Evangelical Congregational Church, of Maynard, Massachusetts, was addressing a full house during his fourth annual Salute to America."

Still another article appeared in the *Beacon* on November 18, 1971, wherein Reverend Gary Heikkila was reported to have stated, "America needs to sing again, celebrate again ... there's too much despair. Let us proudly gather around out flag and all it stands for." This sentiment was reflected in the buoyant attitude of his congregation. Gary had steadily made his two churches newsworthy by his forward movements and his initiative in his sermons and church activities.

It was as early as 1967, during the Vietnamese situation, that an article had announced the first Service of Patriotism that was to be held in both his churches on the following Sunday. It proved to be a huge success, and this service has been continued annually throughout the years. Only two years after Gary had become minister in the Maynard Church on Mission Street and Walnut, the local Maynard newspaper had published an article about it in November of 1968 that began with the heading, "A Church with Conviction." It commended the firm moral stand he had taken in his sermons.

Years later, in the beginning of 1973, Gary decided to make a trip to Hollywood to see his old friends—Zsa Zsa Gabor, Pat Boone, Debbie Reynolds, and others—whom he had known in California. This time, he checked into the Beverly Hills Hotel with no qualms. When he visited her in her home, Zsa Zsa kindly consented to have photos taken with him, which he will always treasure. He called on her in the early evening, and to Gary, her home seemed like a czarina's palace in nineteenth-century Russia. Only Zsa Zsa, Gary thought in pure amazement, could have put this all together with such charming elegance. Perhaps other, more ordinary personalities than Zsa Zsa would have been embarrassed by the glitter, but she seemed only a part of it and not in the least out of place. Greeting him with the title "Father" did not seem inappropriate either. She had a Catholic background, and this was only an honorary title that Gary did not feel he should object to under the circumstances.

From her living room windows, the splendorous view of Los Angeles spread below them to the horizon. And from a room filled with excellent paintings and tapestries, Gary gazed out upon a scene that was fascinating and breathtaking. Several well-trained, beautiful dogs greeted them as they went upstairs to her den, where career mementos of every sort lined the walls. Zsa Zsa moved with the grace of a ballet dancer, captivating him with her chatter, and the visit was thoroughly enjoyable. She was never, despite her sophisticated charisma, anything but a warm, real person with a delightful dialect and the same marvelous beauty off the screen as on.

The Boones, Shirley and Pat, were gracious and charming and made him feel very welcome. And Debbie Reynolds was both enchanting and beautiful and a gracious hostess who also posed for pictures. Others made him feel the charm of Hollywood, but he had no regrets. When the trip was over, he returned to his twin churches, refreshed and happy to continue his chosen life.

In the spring of 1973, the little church in Gardner that he had begun on October 7, 1962 with seven members, including himself, was doing well and was filled to capacity, as was the larger church in Maynard that he had taken over in 1966. After returning from his visit to Hollywood in the spring of 1973, Gary was prepared to carry on with the duties of his two churches by honoring the sixth annual Service of Patriotism coming up that fall. Held on Armistice Day, November 11, 1973, the larger church on Walnut Street in Maynard rang with voices singing "America," and with a short sermon on patriotism that was repeated in the little church in Gardner.

"Perhaps the thirst for spiritual reawakening was at its highest peak," an article about the Maynard church service reported. Leastwise, there appeared among those worshipful members' dignitaries from especially high places in federal, state, and local governments. "Reverend Heikkila said in his sermon," This article informed, "'We have our problems to be sure, but we are still the greatest country in the world. We can best honor America by rededicating ourselves to God.'" This article continued, "He also reaffirmed, 'Our glorious America … one nation under God.' And he declared that 'with spiritual revival we could change our moral atmosphere. We have become so free in our morals that we are no longer free.'"

All in all, God's work—under Reverend Gary Heikkila's direction—was being carried out in a most pleasing way. His mission for the Lord was greatly prospering.

Chapter 20

My Country

A reporter covering the service later wrote: "Reverend Gary Heikkila reminded his listeners that the American people are responding to their obligations to the past, and that the potential for future greatness is being lost in the rush toward self-indulgence." He stated that the country would continue to sink toward eventual destruction if the present all-pervasive apathy of the people was not replaced by a determination to right the wrongs that presently plague society.

In his sermon in the year 1975, to celebrate this service, Reverent Heikkila spoke these words to his congregation:

> We have created the fairest, the most fruitful and the freest nation in the world today ... history has proved that it is harder to keep freedom than to gain it. Many things threaten our freedom today, among them reckless government spending and permissive law enforcement based on monetary resources, handled by greedy, lazy lawyers and judges which in effect punishes society for

> the crimes instead of the criminal. People must wake up to the menaces they have allowed to accumulate. Where are the dependable and honest leaders, willing to make the sacrifices to set an example, to show the way?

But it was a year later, in 1976, that Reverend Heikkila really shocked many of the citizens of the towns of Maynard and Gardner, Massachusetts. He held a purely patriotic celebration in a church.

The populace had previously condoned a little patriotism along with religion in their church, but that year of 1976, the year of the American Bicentennial, the fourth of July fell on a Sunday. And to the amazement of all the townspeople of Maynard except the members of the Mission Evangelical Church, on this beautiful, warm, sunny holiday Sunday morning, they saw all kinds of strangely costumed people—adults and children traversing the streets, all going toward the Mission Evangelical Congregational Church. It was the normal time for church, but they were certainly not properly dressed for church. These people were not dressed in their Sunday best. Instead, they were all dressed up in old-style costumes. Knee britches were worn by small boys and men. The men also wore vests, tri-cornered hats, and buckled shoes, and some even carried powder horns reminiscent of two hundred years ago.

Little girls and women swished along briskly in long, ruffled, Colonial-style dresses; Martha Washington dust caps; shawls; and capes. The traffic officer assigned to duty as usual in that are near the church was truly amazed. He thought he must be dreaming or have gotten his timing wrong. Was there a party somewhere? No. They were all going to a Sunday worship celebration.

But what music was that coming from the church? "My Country 'Tis of Thee." Patriotic music was coming from a church on Sunday morning! It could not be. Was he hearing things, too? Then came "America the Beautiful," which was soon followed by "God Bless America." This was not possible. Where were the fine, old, familiar hymns that always filled the air on Sunday mornings?

Of course, he knew that this was the country's bicentennial celebration of Independence Day. But that would be celebrated in the afternoon at picnics in parks with political speeches and all the holiday accoutrements of the biggest day in America in two hundred years. Surely a church would not be celebrating it like this on Sunday morning! Oh, yes it would. Reverend Gary Heikkila's church would. It was celebrating in just this way, and he had arranged it all. But how did he dare?

Then the traffic policeman heard the powerfully resonant voice of Reverend Heikkila himself booming out through the open door of his church, asking his costumed congregation these questions: "Are we justified in holding a birthday party for our nation in God's house? Would He be impressed by Christians meeting together to celebrate the bicentennial of a nation that is definitely of this world?"

The traffic officer listened in pure amazement. He had never heard of such a thing. Nobody he knew of had ever heard of anything like this—the idea of mixing anything else with religion was unheard of. But as he listened to the words of Reverend Heikkila—who was blessed with a clear, resonant, resounding voice that pleasant to the ear, and who might perhaps be deftly using some of his knowledge of drama—the officer began to wonder if this was really so strange after all.

Perhaps a Christian message was not out of place for a bicentennial or talk of patriotism and love of country not so out of place in a church along with the worship of God. It was just that he'd never heard of it. Nor had others. But the minister of the Mission Evangelical Congregational Church was not doing a really new thing. He was actually doing something that was so very old that the Bible spoke of it.

Reverend Heikkila quoted, "Make a joyful noise," with his sonorous voice ringing out strongly from the crowded church. "It is clear that God had nothing against a celebration that would strike the ears as well as the heart," he declared to his costumed congregation. "We rang our bell in Philadelphia, as the Israelites sounded their trumpets, 'loud and clear.' And the people gathered in churches to hear the Declaration of Independence read. It was a great day—a day to celebrate, that day of liberty, two hundred years ago!" he exhorted.

"Our task is to point our nation toward God, as our forefathers did before us! Our nation was founded by God, and it was to be run under God. Remember that! Our task is to remember the believers who first came to these shores, under the extreme duress of religious persecution. And we must remind those now present in this land what they came here for!

"Each of us, as Christians, must admit that if we fail to do this, we fail both God and Country alike! And remember," He cried to his flock, "a most pertinent line from the book of Psalms, chapter 33, and verse 12: 'Blessed is the nation whose God is the Lord!'" Heikkila was forcefully reminding his congregation in the church of something that most people had long forgotten. The officer nodded in agreement. To him, it made sense.

Soon the short sermon that followed was over, the church service was over, and the "Battle Hymn of the Republic" was being emotionally sung by the entire congregation. It flowed out over the traffic in a magnificent blending of things spiritually harmonious.

Then Reverend Heikkila was greeting his followers at the door as they left, and was seen to be garbed in a strange-looking clerical frock that smacked of a long-ago vintage. White stocks at his throat and a dark cutaway jacket with big gold buttons lent tallness to his fine figure. A black, wide-brimmed parson's hat could well have represented a scene from a church service in 1776, two hundred years ago.

As the people were leaving, the traffic cop could almost hear the words that came into his mind from memory. They were words from Leviticus 25:10: "Proclaim liberty throughout the land unto all the inhabitants thereof." This scene had recalled those words from somewhere deep within the recesses of his mundane mind. As the officer jumped into his cruiser to leave, he asked himself if it really was so strange to bring God's words and God's presence into our worldly events. The men who had framed the Constitution had done this. Maybe that was what he lacked. Maybe we needed God to be closer. Maybe God is interested in our daily lives, not just in our Sunday lives, as most of us have thought for so long—and maybe too long, he mused, as he joined the traffic moving on.

Perhaps Reverend Heikkila had a point, he thought, and he smiled, cruising with the traffic. But the reverend would surely get it from the residents tomorrow, he anticipated, smiling even more. People in New England were not fond of changes. They knew the way things should be, and they should be the way they had always been. He would not want to be in Heikkila's shoes. No, sir—not at all.

Chapter 21

Bicentennial

A storm of censure rained down upon Reverend Gary's head. Not only were he and his two churches castigated by many people of both Maynard and Gardner for what some called his outrageous use of his churches for other than the usual and orthodox purpose that most of the residents thought churches should be used for, but it was also thought that something should be done about it.

He had rushed from the Maynard Church to the smaller church in Gardner to repeat the patriotic services there and had thus invited severe criticism from many people in that small town as well. But Reverend Gary Heikkila was inclined toward bravery. And because of his second talent, he was out of the ordinary. It made of him less an obscure minister to the churches of his parish and made him a more truly Christlike entrepreneur in teaching the Word of God. He made his churches different, as Jesus had made His teaching different.

Jesus had used the regular temples and churches that were already built, but not in the usual way. He did not follow all the ceremonies and pompous rituals that were then in vogue. He spoke as a fellow man who had something to say to fellow men, and He spoke simply. He spoke of the Scriptures as prophecies, as history, as allegoric. He spoke of them in the parables in which they were written—not to be taken literally, but as analogies, as examples and explanations.

Gary did not feel that temples or churches were for limited use and only to present the usual teachings but that they were to be used also for new teaching and different ways of worshipping God, as Jesus' teaching most certainly had been different. So Reverend Heikkila wanted to use his churches for something different in the way of worshipping the Lord, and he wanted to use them not only for the worship of God, but to include, along with that worship of God, the love of country. He felt that churches should be used in the celebration of the freedom of a country that the worshippers loved, as he did. He felt that God loved the goodness of a country as He loved the goodness of mankind, of which a country is made up.

Gary could see no wrong in this and did not feel that celebrating an anniversary of the country they all loved was in any way diminishing to the worship and love that the members of his church felt for God. But others did not see it this way. Still, Gary argued, if it seemed wrong to them to include love of country with the love of Jesus, then he did not agree with those people. It appeared that a good many people saw his point of view and agreed with him.

This was proved by most of his congregation having happily taken part in the wonderful 200th anniversary of the Declaration of Independence of the United States of America. It was further proved by the later congratulations he received from those in high public places who had wished to attend but could not. His unique Bicentennial of Patriotism, held in both the Mission Evangelical Congregational Church in Maynard and the Mission Street Congregational Church in Gardner, Massachusetts, "to reaffirm our faith in America," as he put it, was acclaimed to be a wonderful thing by many who freely congratulated him.

Mayor Stephen J. Erickson of Gardner wrote him a special letter. "Dear Reverend Heikkila: It is with great spiritual enthusiasm that I extend to you my best wishes on this glorious occasion." Pat Boone, the movie actor and longtime friend of Gary during and since Gary's

Hollywood days, wrote in a letter to Gary on that occasion: "Reverend Gary Heikkila: Congratulations, brother! May our loving Lord continue to bless and anoint your ministry and give you harvest. Another Carpenter's helper, Pat Boone."

Gary knew Pat Boone as one of the few faithful followers of Jesus in Hollywood, and Pat had agreed when Gary had said, "Isn't it the Christian's obligation to infiltrate? Should not a true witness for the Lord walk down every avenue? After all, our Lord did not turn from the lepers, from the adulteress. Who will tell these people that salvation is really attainable? Should not a trained witness like myself walk among them and be one with them? God loves these people, too." And with this, Pat had agreed. Though many in Hollywood did not know Gary as a minister, Pat Boone had known. Gary also knew that Billy Graham had ministered to Judy Garland and that he, too, knew Pat Boone as an ardent Christian.

Gary recalled his going to Boone's house for a prayer meeting of the movie stars who were the Boones' special friends. This had to be a clandestine affair and kept between these special people, since a star could not simply go to church; it would create too much of a stir. So only a few knew of Pat and his wife, Shirley's, deep faith. It was very interesting and gratifying, Gary remembered, to see so many well-known actresses and actors there at the prayer meeting in the Boone home.

Years later, some of Gary's own congregation in both Maynard and Gardner were shocked that he would allow his congregation to come to church in costume and that even the minister himself would dare dress in costume as he spoke the Word of God. To them, this seemed coming near to profane. But to those in attendance, it had seemed fine and normal—both devout and patriotic—and they had seen nothing wrong with mixing love of country with their love of God.

Dr. Roberson, President of the Tennessee Schools and pastor of the world-famous Highland Park Baptist Church, after hearing of the event, approved and wrote to the secretary of the Mission Evangelical Church in Maynard, saying, "Please convey my sincere greetings to your pastor, Reverend Russell Gary Heikkila! I rejoice in the ministry that God has given him in your state. I do pray that the richest blessings of God might be upon his ministry." There were many others, including Reverend Billy Graham, who congratulated him. But this did not allay the objections of some to celebrating even the 200th birthday of their beloved country's years of progress.

The message that Gary had conveyed that day in church commemorating the bicentennial anniversary was a short sermon that he called, "The Ram's Horn and the Liberty Bell."

> The United States is two hundred years old today. Throughout the land because the anniversary falls on Sunday preachers are standing before congregations saying in one way or another, with one text or another, "Happy Birthday."
>
> We love this land … But what does God think? This is a Christian church, after all; this is God's house. Are we justified in holding a birthday party for our nation in God's house? Is God in favor of the United States of America or its birthday?
>
> Jesus said, "My kingdom is not of this world." Would he be impressed at Christians meeting together to celebrate the bicentennial of a nation that is definitely of this world? As a matter of fact, I think God celebrates with us this morning, and I think we have proof of that in His Word, the Holy Bible … it is clear from the Scriptures that God loved festivals for His people, whoever and whatever …
>
> God says, in the book of Leviticus, chapter 25, verse 10, "And ye shall hallow the fiftieth year, and proclaim liberty throughout all the land unto all the inhabitants thereof; it shall be a jubilee unto you." Do you notice something familiar? Do these words have a certain ring to them—an American sound to your ears?

> Probably you noticed those familiar words, "Proclaim liberty throughout all the land unto all the inhabitants thereof." Do you realize that those are the very words our founding fathers had inscribed on the Liberty Bell?
>
> "Make a joyful noise unto the world," the Scripture says, so it is clear that God had nothing against a celebration that would strike the ear as well as the heart. He wanted His chosen people to blow a trumpet at that time so that all might appreciate that this festival was indeed special. They used a ram's horn in those days, since they weren't making trumpets as yet, but the noise was real, and it was made in obedience to the direct command from God.

Gary had gone on to say that while the ram's horn is no more, and our clanging, noisy, Liberty Bell is cracked and will no longer ring, we should still remember the ram's horn and the Liberty Bell and never let their memory be lost. Both proclaimed freedom, he reminded his congregation, and also that a celebration was pleasing to God. He also reminded them of the fact that our country was founded under God, and we should not forget it.

He went on further to say, "We should remember those devout believers who came to our shores for freedom from religious persecution. We must always remember what they came here for." He ended on this sincere note and afterwards made an impassioned prayer to the Savior for His blessing upon them all.

Most people thought it was a beautiful sermon. The fact that their church was used for a ceremony to dedicate this one Sunday in two hundred years to a beloved country that God was asked to bless did not seem to them in any way a sin.

Chapter 22

Patriotism

While this had aroused the most notice, the Sunday of July 4, 1976 was not the only celebration Reverend Heikkila had held in his two churches. And while the bicentennial celebration was by far the most ostentatious, he had already celebrated a fourfold even earlier in the year in May of 1976 that was objected to. First, this earlier event celebrated the honor of his own twentieth anniversary as an ordained minister; secondly, he was celebrating the tenth anniversary of his installation as pastor of the Mission Evangelical Congregational Church in Maynard; and third, he celebrated the fourteenth anniversary of his pastorship in the little abandoned church that had stood waiting for him at the end of Mission Street in Gardner.

The fourth event was Reverend Heikkila's own birthday. So being a young-looking forty-four in that year, he had not minded the instance upon this fourth event being added to the multiple-event jubilee that spring in 1976. For this fourfold honoring, his beloved mother and father had both been in attendance. It had added greatly to his happiness that his parents had come to Maynard from his home town in Calumet,

Michigan, near Trimountain, where he was born, and this had made the multiple celebration complete for him.

Greetings and congratulations were received by Gary from Mayor Stephen J. Erickson of Gardner; Dr. Harold Ockenga, pastor of the Park Street Church in Boston; and Dr. Lee Roberson, Chancellor of Tennessee Schools of Chattanooga, Tennessee, from which Gary had been ordained twenty years before. This ordination was one of the fourfold events being celebrated.

Many old friends and associates sent congratulations from near and far, and these, among well wishes and favorable comments, made the day very special for Reverent Heikkila. Following the program that Sunday morning, Gary had met with his parents, Mr. and Mrs. Wallace Heikkila, in the vestry of the church where many friends had gathered around them.

Between his loving parents proudly smiling, the three were pictured in the local paper, the *Assabet Valley Beacon,* on the following Thursday, along with an article titled "Local Dignitaries and Friends Honor Rev. Heikkila," which pleased him and his parents greatly and made this May celebration complete. But it was a year later, in 1977, that Gary had received the highest award for citizenship for his outstanding service and ministry to the city, state, and nation. It was awarded him for his continuing Service of Patriotism that was held annually in his two churches for more than a decade.

In the year 1977, he was also awarded the State Citizenship Medal by the state VFW at their state convention. The Veterans of Foreign Wars furthermore presented to him in 1977 the Disabled American Veterans Distinguished Service Award. The year 1977 had begun auspiciously for Rev. Heikkila with his being the principal speaker for the annual Voice of Democracy Awards Dinner on February 19, sponsored by the Veterans of Foreign Wars. Later, on June 18, Gary had received a Citizenship Medal from the VFW. Still later in that year, he also received the Distinguished Service Award.

Gary's outstanding achievements were noted in Washington, DC by Father Robert F. Drinan from the House of Representatives, who wrote, "Dear Reverend Heikkila: I was quite pleased to learn that you have been honored by the Veterans of Foreign Wars for your superb leadership, patriotism, and religious faith. Your life and teachings have inspired many people to great achievement. I am sure you will continue to instill patriotism and religious learning throughout our nation in the years ahead. I wish you good luck on that mission, and again, I want to extend my congratulations. With every best wish."

Gary also received congratulations for this tenth annual Service of Patriotism in November of 1977. It was in the form of a personal letter from the Governor of California, Ronald Reagan, which read,

> As Governor of California, I am pleased to join in your service of patriotism.
>
> Freedom is a fragile thing and is never more than one generation from extinction. It is not ours by inheritance. It must be defended constantly by each generation for it comes only once to a people. Those who have known freedom and then lost it have never known it again.
>
> The light of freedom, the basic tenet on which America was founded, has been kept burning bright these many generations by men of vision and courage, and the torch has now been passed to us. We have the responsibility of guarding and passing it on to future generations as they are ready to take and protect it.
>
> We give thanks to God that we are a part of a nation dedicated to freedom and liberty for all.

In that tenth annual Service of Patriotism, held in both churches in November of 1977, Gary also gave a sermon that impressed the entire congregation and the newspapers with his prophesy. He warned of imminent destruction in the way the world was headed at that time. His prognosis was concerned both with the people personally and politically. His prediction was drastic but not unbelievable by thinking people, and the title of his sermon was "The Nation's Hope." In it, he warned that our nation could well suffer the fate of Babylon as described in Revelations and be destroyed in an hour.

He concluded, "I feel there is something about our country that suggests the destruction of Babylon; when all the glorious wealth of Babylon was laid waste in one hour. All of the glorious wealth of our largest cities today—our wonderful high buildings, our marvelous bridges, our banks and all they contain, our homes, our children, and ourselves—will all be laid waste in three seconds after a modern hydrogen bomb hits us."

Yet he gave some hope. "But even then, our souls can be saved, if we are ready. Many will not be ready. But we could stop it all now, if we cared more for God than for money or possessions—but we don't, and we won't. We will be destroyed, as Babylon was, and for the same reason."

He did not stop there. He went on to explain, "The bomb dropped on Hiroshima was the equivalent of thirteen thousand tons of TNT. The Soviet equivalent now, in 1977, is 5.4 billion tons. While our own is 4.2 billion tons … We are still behind the Soviet nation in our tonnage, counted in billions now instead of the scanty thousands that wiped out two Japanese cities that were as large as most of ours.

"But this is only 1977, and we are escalating, and so are the Russians," he continued. "It is a game played with lives, but there is much money in it. And that is exactly what made the temples of Jerusalem so rich and so powerful. Not much has changed except size in these two thousand years. Our temples are even large, and are also very rich … How can we save ourselves?" he asked.

"Christian people who live in the great nations of the world must understand the directions their government is taking and must make sure they do not go along with the abominations that everyone else engages in—personal as well as political," he cautioned.

"But we all say, 'Government is too big—too inclusive. What can we do?' And because we feel helpless and government seems so big, so powerful, many people have made government their God and have forgotten their Maker.

"'How can we resist this evil?' they ask. The answer is found in the gospel of salvation of the Lord Jesus Christ, who said, 'Woe to the nation which turns against the church of the Lord Jesus Christ. A nation which neglects, or hinders the Christian Church in any way renders itself subject to the judgment of God.' The greatest message of the entire Bible is salvation; which God offers us in the Lord Jesus Christ. In Him, is the salvation that will bring to our nation the true glory it desires."

"But a host of ominous signs on the immediate horizon indicate that Armageddon is near," he warned. How near? Very near. America's hope? A truly Holy Spirit awakening across this land could save our souls, at least—and perhaps, who knows, save our nation as well." Gary's pause here had allowed his words to be absorbed in the silence in which they were received.

"When it is realized," he continued, "that today, we are even further under the threat of hydrogen bombs that can wipe out New York or any major city in three seconds and leave utter devastation, with nowhere to hide from the poisonous fumes; we see that Jesus, through the Holy Scriptures, tried to warn us of our fate. And unless we turn around and follow God's will instead of our own, we bring our fate upon us.

"When America ceases to follow God's will—God's program of Bible morality—America will experience what many nations have experienced in the history of the world up until this very day ... and today will follow yesterday, and our beloved nation will follow its fate brought on by corruption, as others before us have done." He said this sadly, and none of those who were there could fail to receive his message.

Some who heard that stirring sermon heeded his words for themselves and turned to God for their salvation. Others went on, as humanity does—uncaring, unaware, vulnerable, and unknowing in their sublime ignorance of their Maker and of their fate. But while Gary had found his place in life, no life is spared the sorrow of loss of loved ones.

It was then, three years later, on a Sunday morning in 1980, October 5, after Gary had held his earlier services at the Evangelical Church in Maynard and had driven to Gardner and was preparing to step into the Mission Street Church there at 11:00 a.m. that word arrived of his mother's sudden death. It was totally unexpected, as she had seemed to be in good health. His mother and father were inseparable, but he could not save her. She had slipped quietly away in the early morning of a massive heart attack.

Gary was hardly able to conduct his services before making a plane for Calumet to join in mourning with his grieving father and sister. On the plane, it was all Gary could do to keep from breaking down when he remembered how many times as a child he had thought, "I have the most beautiful mother in the world." There had always been a close and special bond between them.

When he arrived in Calumet and was with his remaining loved ones, they tried to comfort each other. They were grateful that she had gone so peacefully, and while they suffered a deep loss and would miss her always, they appreciated having had her for at least this long. She was, they felt, the best wife and mother in the whole world. She had a mother's heart, a mother's sensitivity, and love that encompassed all, and her loss was deeply grieved.

She was buried in Mountain View Cemetery in South Range, near Trimountain, and Gary felt emptiness in his heart that would never be filled. It had been a comfort to him that Rev. Rodney Johnson, his parents' pastor, had read the passages of resurrection assurances from the Scriptures. "Because I live, ye shall live also" (John 14:19). "I am the resurrection, and the life; he that believeth in me, though he were dead, yet shall he live" (John 11:25). Gary's heart said in gratitude, "Praise be to God."

He also was grateful for the presence of Reverend Jack Oiva Rosenberg; a friend who seemed was there by divine appointment, since he had happened to be visiting in Calumet at that fateful hour. He prayed comfortingly at the church. Gary also appreciated the presence of Mrs. Elsie Chipman, a dear family friend for many years who had been like a sister to Gary's mother.

The emptiness and sorrow in Gary's heart would always remain, but he was comforted by the knowledge of the resurrection and its glorious promise. While deep grief has remained, he will always give thanks for his father, sister, and dear friends who gave him comfort. Gary's sermons gave them comfort, too, and his messages were many and varied as the days went on after he had returned home with great sorrow in his heart. The quality of his sermons seemed only to increase with time.

He attracted many different kinds of people by his perceptive and relevant interpretations of the Bible and by his sincere interest in those who came to listen. His help is always offered, and he is respected and loved in both his parishes and in the communities in which they reside, where he has offered a helping hand to many.

He helped a young concert pianist and recording artist, Paul Heffron, a graduate of the Boston Conservatory of Music, who specializes in writing contemporary songs based upon the Scripture. Paul had recorded an album in Nashville, writing his own lyrics and music. His debut album, *I Love You, Jesus,* was very popular, and Gary, as busy as he was with two churches to attend, went on speaking engagements with him to introduce him, assist him in his career, and help him sell his album. Gary became his concert program coordinator and befriended him in every way. He took great pride in the talented young man's progress.

Gary's good intentions were not always appreciated. He was active as chaplain of the Concord District court and also of the Maynard Police Department, and one of his younger parishioners had become interested in a young man who unfortunately drank heavily. She had persuaded him to attend church and AA meetings, but he still drank. After a heavy bout, he threatened to kill his divorced wife and their young children. The girl broke off with him, but he subsequently drank even more heavily and went to the length of stealing a car. This had landed him in the Billerica correctional facility.

Since he had previously attended church services and had become acquainted with Reverend Gary Heikkila, he felt entitled, because of this and his belief in Gary's kindness, to call upon him to provide money for bail. Gary considered it but was advised by the probation department of the Concord District Court not to give the money. When he refused, the man threatened to kill him.

The prisoner was also discovered to have spent time in the Michigan State Prison for extortion and robbery and was considered to be dangerous. But Gary did not worry about this and was determined to help him all he could. The man claimed his problems were of a neurological nature, but an examination by the state hospital pointed more to a serious drinking problem.

Before final trial came up, he was sent to the Bridgewater State Hospital for evaluation and then released for trial. Bail was allowed and produced by a bondsman with the condition that the accused man stay away from the people he had threatened to kill, which included Reverent Heikkila. Because of his drinking habits, it was felt that he might not obey these orders and that Gary's life was in danger. Gary, however, carried on his duties as if there was nothing amiss, and while others feared for him, he had no fear for himself.

The man jumped bail, and those around Gary lived in fear. However, the man remained a fugitive and never returned, though officials were watchful for a long time. This unduly excited some of the church members, who were worried about the activity on the officials' part concerning their pastor. But Gary suffered no ill effects.

There were others whom Gary helped, however, who did appreciate his efforts to assist people in trouble. One of them was a young woman who was fearful and timid. She was alone and felt herself to be a misfit in life. Her only pleasure was in the words she heard from Reverend Heikkila on Sunday mornings. She confessed that while she worked all week, she looked forward only to that. The sermons gave her comfort. His unfailing "See you Sunday" was an invitation she would not pass up, and she became a faithful member of the church.

Her nature, though she was young, had become embittered because of an abusive family, and her thoughts were often on suicide. She was a recluse who went out of her room only to work and on Sunday mornings to listen to the Reverend Heikkila speak. Then on Sunday, the words in one of his sermons reached her and sank deep into her anxious mind the message that "There is nothing in your life that is not removable by the almighty power of God!" These words struck a chord in the mind of the timid young girl.

Miraculously, her wounds began to heal. Her mind and spirit began to grow. She changed and became no longer afraid. Her natural sweetness of character began to emerge. She eventually became a happy person.

In speaking of him later, she likened Gary to Jesus, in that she described him thus: "He is a man humble and true; of a kindly, patient, gentle nature; a gallant heart; strong, though gentle; firm in the right, and staunch against evil. He is tender and sensitive to the hurts of others, and his warm smile offers Christ's forgiveness."

It follows that if he has saved one person from a life of bitterness and fear, how many others have his messages saved? He is able to explain the Bible's messages so that they seem clear, warm, and friendly, not cold and threatening, as many ministers do. He is a beloved pastor of his churches and a beloved man to those within his parishes. One friend calls him "a prince of the King," and indeed he may so be called.

Another person whom he had helped is a young man who declares the feeling that Gary is a true reflection of Jesus. He says of Reverent Heikkila, "If his love for people was not real, it would have cracked a thousand times." The young man has also said, "I needed him, and he was there. He listens to people, and he helps them. I feel the presence of Jesus in this man of God, and I feel when I'm with him, almost as if I were with Jesus Himself."

In further expression, this young man explained, "I knew, the first time I listened to Reverend Heikkila, that he had a message from God for me. And from him I learned how God wishes me to be. And I try. I want to please God." Then, thoughtfully, he added, "Reverend Heikkila inspires me to love God through Jesus. I know the reverend has suffered, too, but he tells me he had learned a great deal by his experiences and has drawn closer to God and to Jesus, whom he truly loves. He is my inspiration. I think he knows firsthand some of the suffering that humanity, in its callousness and ignorance, not to mention the evilness of men, imposed upon his beloved Jesus when he, too, walked upon this earth." In this tribute is perhaps the essence of the deep love and respect that many in all walks of life have felt for this man whom the Lord has called upon to serve Him.

Epilogue

Though Gary himself is all too human, he can inspire good in others, as Jesus has inspired good in him. He can impart his faith to others. His faith tells him that God loves everyone, even as he knows God loves him, and for this love, Gary is ever grateful.

Many consider his sermons to be works of art. And how could he do this without the dramatic talent he possesses? God gave him that talent, and now he has put it to use for the Lord. Those who know Gary love him and go back again and again to hear what he has to say. He can make the Bible's message meaningful and vital.

Gary's life is (and has been for many years) an example of God's will. His patience, forbearance, stability, and perseverance provide a noble example of obeying God's will and staying true to Jesus' love for His fellow men. Gary has given both his talents to the Lord, and God has blessed him a hundred fold.

There are many who love Dr. Gary Heikkila and praise the Lord for his inspiring and Christ-exalting ministry. Dr. W. A. Criswell, author of thirty books, spent half a century in the ministry. He is the pastor of the First Baptist Church of Dallas, Texas and knows Gary well.

Dr. Criswell attended the Diamond Jubilee held in Gary Heikkila's Mission Evangelical Congregational Church in Maynard in December of 1981 and later wrote him a note addressed, "My precious friend, Gary Heikkila." The gist of the note was accompanied by the words,

"You do things in a beautiful way." And in closing, he said warmly, "You are a friend of friends." There is no way that Gary can express his heartfelt devotion to such a friend but to feel deep love in his heart.

Dr. Billy Graham congratulated Gary on the Diamond Jubilee year of his church in Massachusetts. Edward King, former Governor of Massachusetts, sent him a personal letter from the State House in Boston, commending him and congratulating him on his annual Honor America Day with his Service of Patriotism held at his two churches and sent Gary a personal greeting.

Pat Boone from Hollywood sent personal congratulations, as did several other well-known actresses and actors of longstanding friendship, including Miss Zsa Zsa Gabor and others, with sincere congratulations for his annual Service of Patriotism. Mr. Allen C. Emery, a friend and the President of the Billy Graham Evangelistic Association, sent a personal letter to Gary. From the Tennessee Temple Schools in Chattanooga, Tennessee, where Gary was ordained so many years ago, a warm and friendly letter from the founder and Chancellor, Dr. Lee Roberson, brought joy to Gary's life. With such friends as these over the years who mean so much to him, he persevered and made them proud, as he is proud to know them.

Gary will not forget or even cease to love that little group of six who were the founders of his first little church on Mission Street in Gardner on October 7, 1962. Arlie and Lil Wiita, Mrs. Valija Balins, Mrs. Elsie Chipman, Mr. Onnie Herk, and Mrs. Eva Couture will never be forgotten or cease to be blessed.

Gary still preaches the simple and sincere gospel to hundreds more in his larger ministry beyond the walls of the Gardner and Maynard churches. And he still stretches out his hand to all who need him. He is a talented, devoted, complex, and able man. He is a sincere man who feels much, lives quietly, and devotes his life to serving the Lord God Christ.

He loves deeply, and his devotion to his beloved Jesus is demonstrated not only in his sermons, but also in his life.

If God has more use for him, he is ready to expand his potential. If He can find more use for Gary, Gary is ready, willing, and able, and may he go forth to conquer further with God's greatest blessing upon him.

Highlights of Dr. Gary Heikkila's Continuing Ministry

On October 5, 1982, in honor of Rev. Gary Heikkila's twentieth anniversary with Mission Street Church, a celebration for God's glory took place in the Honorable Fred E. Perry Auditorium in Gardner. The public was invited. We welcomed guest speaker Rick Stanley, Elvis Presley's stepbrother, who was a ministerial student at the Criswell Center for Biblical Studies in Dallas, Texas.

By the time the church's ninetieth anniversary arrived, Mission Street Church had brought in many new believers through Pastor Heikkila's reach-out crusades and live radio broadcasts over WGAW in Gardner. The morning service has been broadcast live for over twenty-five years in the tri-state area.

Again, the congregation was ready to celebrate God's blessings. On September 5, 1984, a praise service was held, with many area churches represented. Dr. Paige Patterson, president of Criswell Center for Biblical Studies and Associate pastor at the First Baptist Church, Dallas, Texas was invited as special guest speaker. Another special guest, Rico Petrocelli, former Red Sox all-star shortstop, and Bob Clinkscale, TV and radio personality from Channel 5, brought in people from all walks of life. Paul Heffron was a special musical guest. Pastor Heikkila was celebrating his twenty-second anniversary as undershepherd.

On October 3, 1987, Pastor Heikkila's twenty-fifth year with Mission Street Church, a silver anniversary celebration was held. R. Gary Heikkila faithfully reached out by rightfully dividing God's Word and sharing it with the city of Gardner and surrounding areas. Bob Clinkscale, Channel 5 anchorman, was invited as master of ceremonies. Pastor Heikkila received a proclamation for his religious and civil accomplishments issued by Gov. Michael Dukakis. The address was presented by Rev. Keijo I. Aho of Quincy, Massachusetts, a close friend and yoke-fellow in the pilgrimage.

When Pastor Heikkila had a message to deliver, nothing deterred him from his commitment to our Lord Jesus Christ. Sometimes he traveled through major snowstorms to preach. Other times, like Easter sunrise services at the Cathedral of the Pines in Rindge, New Hampshire, he spoke in the midst of lightly falling rain with almost two thousand worshippers! Each November for twenty-seven years, Pastor Heikkila has honored our country's veterans by bringing them hope through God's Word during a service of patriotism in both his Maynard parish, Mission Evangelical Congregational Church, and in Gardner.

Community service is not overlooked by this minister, as he conducted services for many years in the Walden House Healthcare Nursing Home in Concord, Massachusetts. This committed man of the gospel also served as chaplain of the Maynard Police Department and was chaplain of the Concord District Court.

God shined down with his outpouring of blessings for this loyal minister. Pastor Heikkila received numerous awards and commendations from civil, fraternal, and patriotic organizations, including the highest award given to a civilian by the Massachusetts Veterans of Foreign Wars, the State Citizenship medal.

On February 10, 1991, Pastor Heikkila had preached and ministered for twenty-five years in sister church Mission Evangelical Congregational

Church in Maynard, Massachusetts. During this service, he was awarded the Doctor of Divinity by the Triune Biblical University of Kelso, Washington. It was conferred by Dr. Mildred Fay Jefferson, surgeon with the Boston University Medical Center.

From the dignitaries in Washington, the Commonwealth of Massachusetts, and across the United States, Dr. Heikkila opened letters congratulating him as a religious leader and committed and faithful servant of God. President George Bush wrote, "In your work as a religious leader, you have helped people draw closer to our creator and to one another. You have helped them gain the spiritual strength and peace of mind that are often elusive but always needed in a very challenging world."

On May 21, 1994, he was invited to bring the address at Triune Biblical University Spring Commencement. Another degree, the Doctor of Literature Degree, was presented to Dr. R. Gary Heikkila by the university at this time.

After returning home to his two churches, this dedicated man moved forward, calling others to come to the Lord Jesus Christ in repentance and faith. In the darkest night, people would remember his messages—messages that Christ Himself had spoken to the multitudes. Two small churches had become known as lighthouses for the gospel.

When October 4, 1994 arrived, Chestnut Street Methodist Church opened their doors in honoring Mission Street Congregational Church, Gardner for its founding and hundredth anniversary. Dr. W. A. Criswell, Billy Graham's pastor from the world-famed First Baptist Church in Dallas, Texas, brought a dynamic message and reminded everyone of Dr. Heikkila's thirty-second year as this little church's undershepherd. Greetings were read from President Bill Clinton, Governor Bill Weld, Senator Ted Kennedy, and a variety of dignitaries. The mayor, Charles Manca, graciously read proclamations to the church and Dr. Heikkila.

What God has begun, He will bring to fruition. Dr. R. Gary Heikkila set the theme for the hundredth year and the future: "Run the race." The theme is from Hebrews 12:1: "Let us run with endurance the race that is set before us." That is a call to Christian living. And if you look beyond that verse to the next one, you'll see the *source* of our Christian life: "Jesus, the author and finisher of our faith," or in the words of another translation, "Jesus, on whom our faith depends from the beginning to end." *We can depend on Him.* He died for our salvation. He rose from the dead that we might have eternal life. He is with us, as He promised, always—even to the end of time.

Having struggled so long ago with the possibilities of a Hollywood career, R. Gary Heikkila has been faithful in communicating the gospel by command performance for the King of kings and Lord of lords. Christ Jesus, by His outrageous grace, continues to turn Heikkila's sunset to sunrise, his tears into telescopes, and his Calvary into Easter.

Postscript

Having read my story, I pray you will seek God's perfect will for your life as you walk this pilgrim journey. I am convinced that the greatest formula for living a successful and abundant life is found in Matthew 6:33: "But seek first the kingdom of God and His righteousness, and all these things will be added to you."

I am convinced now, more than ever, that Christ alone is God's answer to life's deepest problems. Jesus Christ is God's unique Son and was sent from heaven to save us from our sins. I suppose the most famous verse in the Bible is John 3:16: "For God so loved the world that He gave His only begotten Son, that whosoever believes in Him should not perish but have everlasting life." We are born into the family of God when we are willing to repent of our sins and accept Jesus Christ as Savior—plus nothing, minus nothing. He has the power to forgive our sins and give us eternal life through faith in His finished work on the blood-splotched cross. The great purpose for which our Savior came into the world has been finished (John 19:30, Isaiah 53:11). God in His grace invites us to receive Jesus into our lives as our personal Lord and Savior (Acts 16:31, Romans 10:9–10, John 14:6). Salvation is found only in the person of Jesus Christ. He who has Jesus Christ has life, and conversely, he who is without Jesus Christ has no life (1 John 5:12).

A man is poor, ragged, and hungry if he has the whole world and does not know the Lord. "For what profit is it to a man if he gains the whole world, and loses his own soul? Or what will a man give in exchange for his soul?" (Matthew 16:26). But his life is blessed beyond compare if he knows and loves the blessed Jesus!

Would you have the blessed assurance of the forgiveness of your sins and the promise of everlasting life? With my deepest soul, I invite you to pray this prayer: "Dear Jesus, believing that I am a sinner and that you died on the cross for my sins, please forgive me of my sins and come into my heart as my Lord and Savior. If you will help me, I am willing to repent of my sins and surrender my life to you right now. In Jesus' name I pray. Amen."

Publisher's Review

It is our privilege to have been involved in the production of this eminent writing achievement by Dr. R. Gary Heikkila. May I take the liberty to mention two statements by the author? These statements seem to give a starting and an ending place in which this exciting drama takes place.

1. "I went to Hollywood for the best Christian reason. I wanted to play the part of Jesus Christ. It began an incredible journey that turned into a journey independent of God. Like others who have heard the call of the Master, our paths of righteousness are not always in a straight line but are often detoured into the far-off city, like the prodigal of old."
2. "From Hope Street in Hollywood to Mission Street in Gardner was an unforgettable journey! Through it all, I learned the most significant fact of my life. No matter how far a man may go from God, the Father is always waiting with open arms to welcome him back. For almost four decades, my stage has been pulpit-size. From it I have discovered meaning, purpose, and fulfillment."

Some will find it easy to identify with Gary as he leads them through his exciting experiences. Many of us no doubt will see a picture of ourselves as he writes of college days, his big moments in the movie industry, and his war days in Korea. I find it incredible that through all these life events, God's calling was so strong and meaningful.

I know you will agree that this book is one of the best of its kind. May you recommend it to others so that they too will enjoy this wonderful reading experience.

Leroy Mikels, ThD, TBU Publishers and

President of Triune Biblical University

Appendix

My Journey to Greece

Having just returned from a preaching mission in Greece, I am still living in the afterglow of visiting the various places of antiquity that are so filled with biblical and secular history.

I was invited by the Reverend John Yphantidis, pastor of the thriving and spiritually healthy Green Evangelical Church in Katerini, to be one of many speakers in their long tradition of exciting and renowned conferences. Fortunately, my Greek translator, Jeff Baldwin, was President of the Greek Bible School. Learning to speak in brief sentences was a new experience for me and one that I hope did not set the convocation back fifty years!

When I think of Greece, I immediately think of the anointed ministry of the apostle Paul. St. John Chrysostom said of St. Paul, "If diamond became gold and gold diamond, then we should be able to give an image of the soul of Paul. But why compare him with diamond and gold? Put the whole world on one side of the scale and you will see that the soul of Paul outweighs it."

Once a fanatical persecutor of the Christians (Galatians 1:13–14; Acts 8:3; 9: 2; 26:9–11), Paul (his Jewish name was Saul), after his conversion on the Damascus Road (Acts 9:3–6; Acts 22, 26), embraced the Christian faith and devoted the rest of his life to his missionary journeys. In a series of journeys throughout the Mediterranean basin, he succeeded in carrying the Christian message outside the borders of Greece to Italy and Spain. The apostle Paul, having now believed in Christ with his heart and mind, set a new and single purpose in his life—the preaching of Christianity (2 Timothy 1, 11). His love for Christ and the unshakeable conviction that he had been commissioned by Christ were his weapons in the face of dangers, deprivation, and persecution (2 Corinthians 11:22–31, 2 Timothy 4:7–8).

My whirlwind tour of Corinth, Philippi and Thessaloniki, Athens, Troas, Kavala, and Berea (modern Veria) was marvelous in the extreme. My Greek host and guide was Vasa Filios, a remarkable and godly woman who could easily win the Indianapolis 500 as she drove through many narrow and heart-stopping streets.

Among the many historical sites I visited, I felt personally moved as I came to Troas. It was on this spot, the meeting place between Greece and the East, that Paul's vision to the cities of Greece was ordained by God (Acts 16:9). This vision, just like the call on the Damascus road, proved of decisive importance for the spread of Christianity. Without loss of time, Paul made ready to go to Greece, knowing that the time had come for the message to be preached in the home of the ancient Green religion.

When visiting Philippi, one is reminded even today of the former grandeur of the Roman city. Phillip II, King of Macedonia, discerning the economic and strategic importance of the city, captured and fortified it and gave it his name—Philippi. Paul would have probably entered the city by its eastern gate, the so-called Neapolis Gate. Paul stayed in

Philippi for a number of days. His first concern was to make contact with Jews living there. However, nowhere do we find any mention of a synagogue. Paul left the city and made his way to the river bank, where they gathered to pray. It was here that Lydia, a seller of textiles form Thyatira in Asia Minor, became the first woman to be baptized on European soil (Acts 16:12–15). With my companions, Marianthie Gossios and Irene Lamb, we visited the archaeological site of Philippi. There is a small river—a "little Jordan," as it has been called—where it is believed that the baptism of Lydia took place. A small Greek Orthodox church was erected on the spot in memory of the event. This place received the name of Lydia. The fresco on the ceiling of the church suggests that Christ was immersed rather than sprinkled upon, as many other paintings suggest.

I was deeply moved to visit St. Paul's prison. According to tradition, St. Paul is believed to have been imprisoned here. It is actually a Roman water cistern that was later converted into a place of worship. After the triumph of Christianity, Philippi developed into a major city of strategic importance. In the Byzantine period, a large number of Christian monuments were erected. To the present day, the ruins of no fewer than four early Christian basilicas can be seen on the archaeological site of Philippi.

We visited Thessalonica (modern Thessaloniki), and I was amazed to discover that the churches make up a veritable treasure house of Christian art, covering all phases of the Byzantine age. Today, Thessaloniki, the Bride of the Thermaic, has the second-largest population in Greece. It is without dispute that St. Paul cultivated the first seed of the new religion in Thessaloniki. His first concern was to make contact with the local Jewish synagogue (Acts 17:2–4). Much light is shown on the content of Paul's preaching in Thessaloniki by the book of Acts and the two letters to the Thessalonians. His central themes were the passion and resurrection of Christ and His second coming. He urged believers to be vigilant, since they would give an account of themselves before Christ. He stressed that the hour of judgment would come after the appearance of the Antichrist (2 Thessalonians 2:2–5).

Paul chose to preach Christianity in Athens—the cradle of civilization and of the ancient Greek religion. Athens in the time of the apostle Paul was not, of course, the flourishing city of the Classical period, but it still retained some measure of the glory of the past and its numerous monuments. Paul was outraged to see the city so full of idols (Acts 17:16–17). There are not words to describe the awesome and overwhelming site of the stunning Parthenon on the Acropolis! The Acropolis was the place where the worship of Athena, the city's most important deity, developed. Seeing the Parthenon bathed in light at night and the sun in the morning is beyond description! It dominates the center of the city.

Dr. Heikkila in front of the Parthenon on the Acropolis in Athens, Greece.

Dr. Heikkila on a preaching mission in Katerini, Greece.

Dr. Heikkila in Philippi, standing at the entrance where, according to tradition, the prison of St. Paul was located.

Dr. Gary Heikkila portrays Gardner's first minister, the Rev. Jonathan Osgood, in a special cemetery reenactment held as part of the 225th anniversary of the founding of the City of Gardner, Massachusetts. The reenactment took place in the cemetery behind the First Congregational Church that replaced Gardner's first Meeting House. By popular demand, the event was held for a second time on September 18, 2010.

The Spiritual Adventure Continues

The Rev. Dr. Russell Gary Heikkila celebrated the fifth-sixth anniversary of his ordination to the ministry on May 25, 2012. He was ordained in the historic First Baptist Church of Chattanooga, Tennessee, on May 25, 1956, by Dr. Lee Roberson and members of the ordination council, including Dr. Charles Weigle, who wrote the famous hymn, "No One Ever Cared for Me like Jesus."

Dr. Heikkila also celebrates fifty years of ministry to the City of Gardner and in New England. He began his ministry in Gardner, following a New England speaking tour for the National Association of Evangelicals (having jettisoned a Hollywood career), on October 7, 1962, at Mission Street Congregational Church, off West Street, in Gardner. Ironically, a study of church records revealed that the church was incorporated on October 7, 1894! He served "The Little Church around the Corner" for thirty-five years.

Heikkila has been described as a pastor who has a multiplicity of gifts. He has been considered the mentor to many young pastors. His selfless ministry in Christ has been inspiring, fruitful, and worthy, and pleasing to the Lord.

His conservative, biblical preaching has been an inspiration to people of all faiths and denominations. His zeal and enthusiasm in proclaiming the Word of God throughout his long ministry is legend.

For several decades, Heikkila also proclaimed the gospel to a large radio audience over WGAW. The weekly Sunday morning worship celebration brought comfort, hope, and strength to the unchurched, and to those unable to attend services because of health issues.

For twenty-nine years, Dr. Heikkila conducted a far-farmed "Service of Patriotism," reminding countless multitudes of the high price which this country paid for the freedom and liberties which it enjoys. The VFW honored Heikkila with its highest civilian award, the *State Citizenship Medal* on June 18, 1977. Many honors and accolades have been paid him over the years.

Heikkila has served as a Juvenile Court Chaplain in Concord, a Hospice Chaplain in Gardner, and a Police Chaplain in Maynard. He is currently a Certified Master Chaplain, CMC, for Homeland Security and a Minister-at-Large.

He has been named Pastor Emeritus of three of his former parishes: Mission Street Congregational Church of Gardner; Mission Evangelical Congregational Church of Maynard; and the Elm Street Community church of Fitchburg. Heikkila also serves as

Associate Pastor at the Elm Street Community Church.

Heikkila's ministry could be summed up in the words of St. Paul in I Timothy 1:12: "I am grateful to Christ Jesus…because He judged me faithful and appointed me to his service…"

CPSIA information can be obtained at www.ICGtesting.com
Printed in the USA
BVOW032035210213

313909BV00002B/30/P

9 781449 767808